AF478887

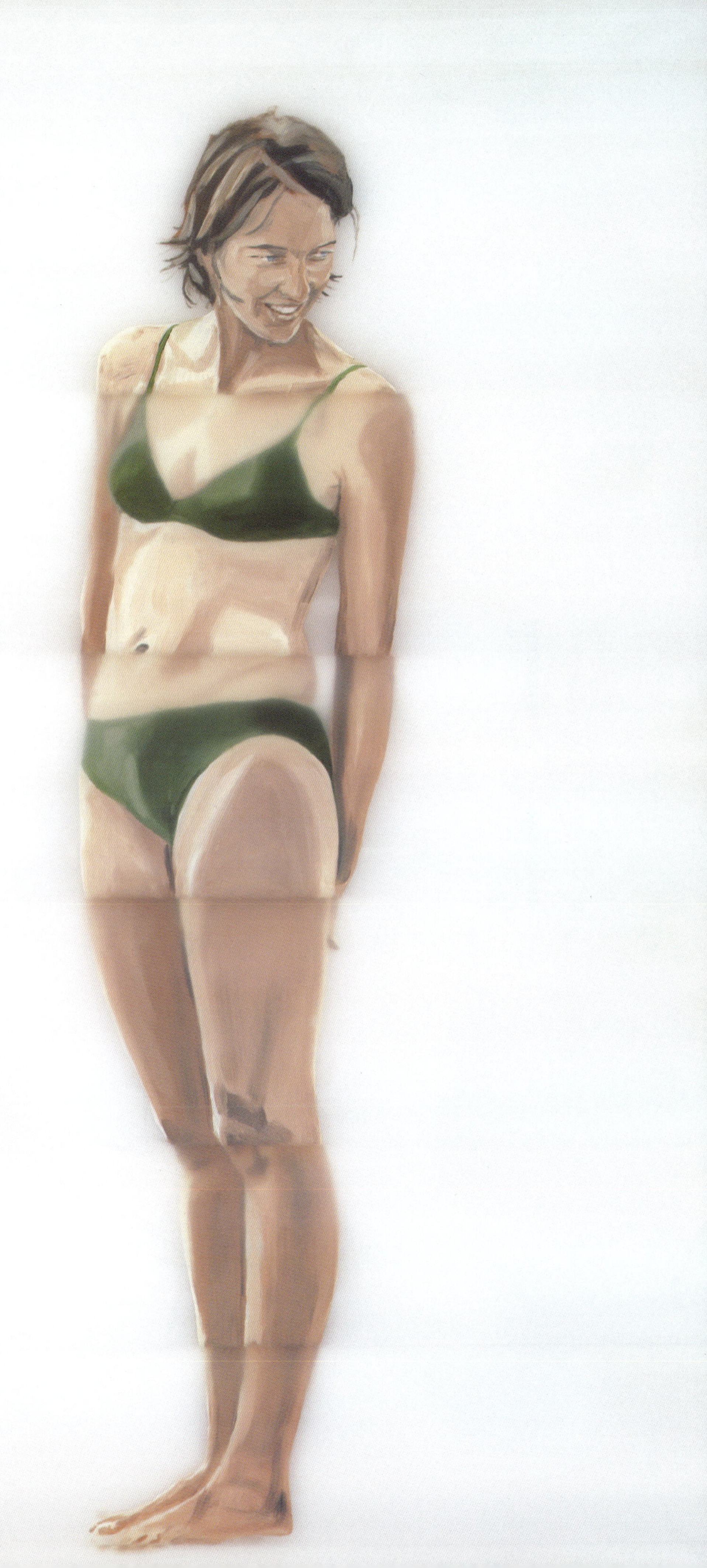

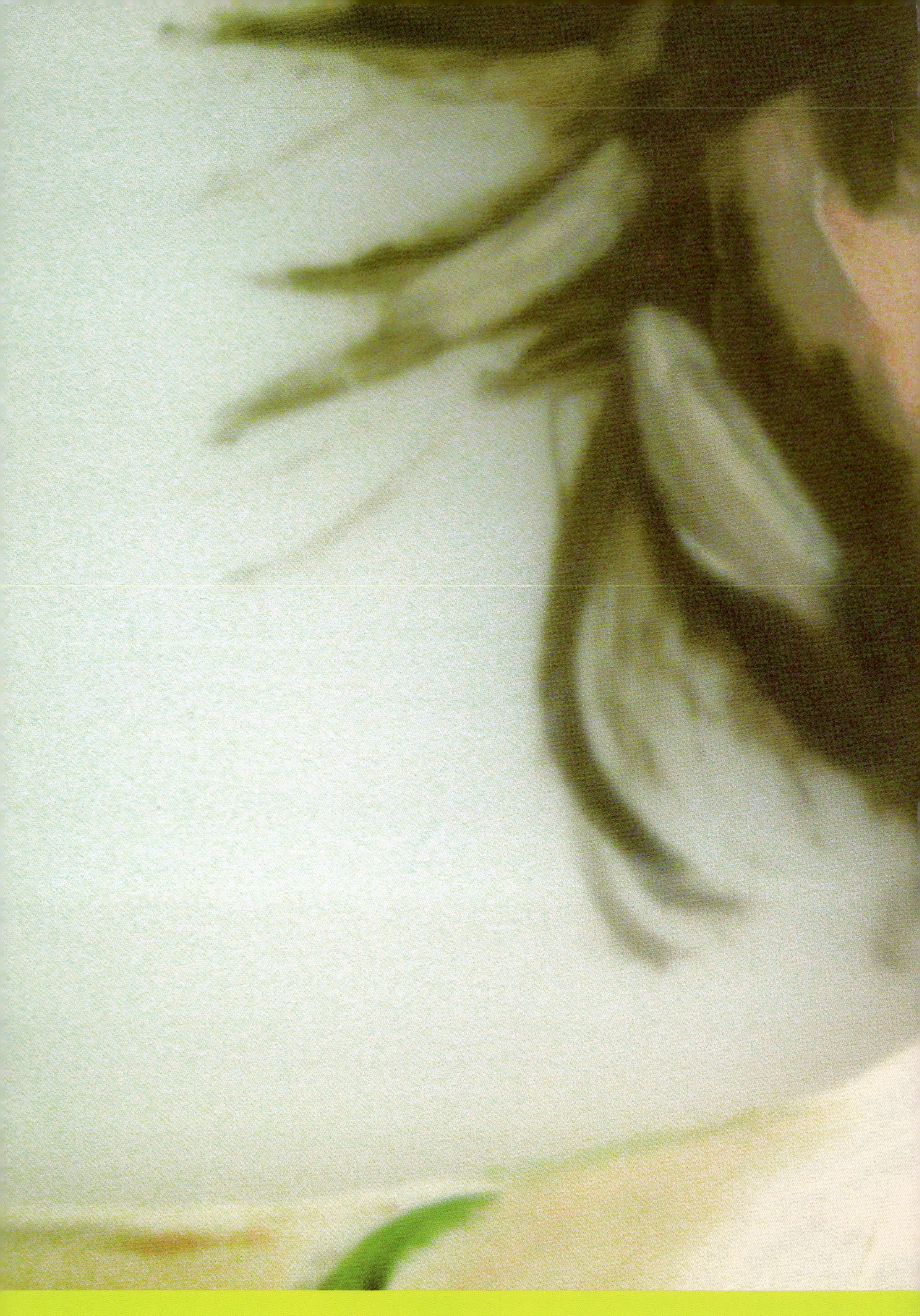

Katharina

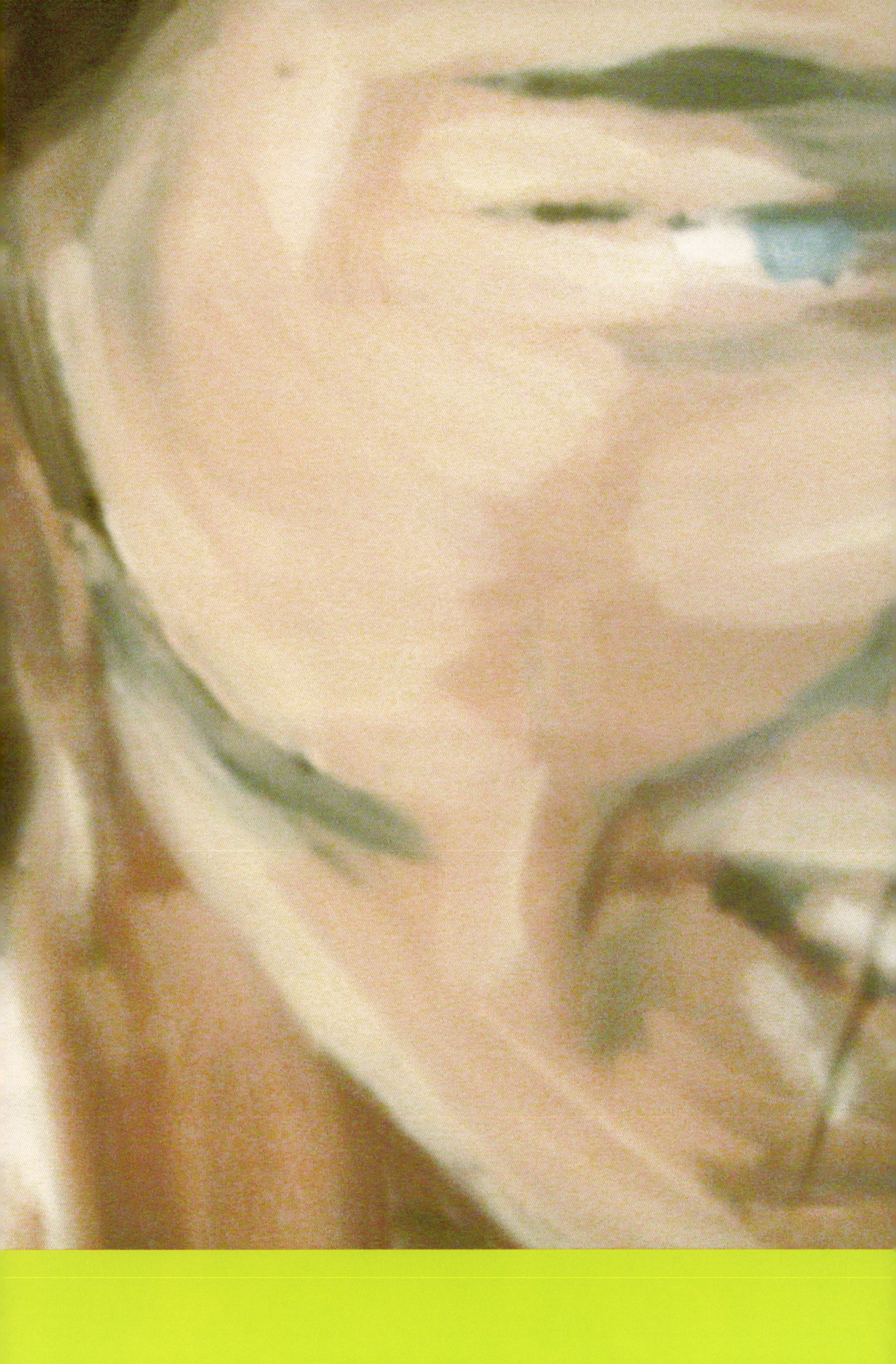

Introductory text by **Richard Dailey**
Interview by **Benedikt Ledebur**
A letter to Sébastien by **Erwin Wurm**

onestar press monos

Sébastien de Ganay

portraits & sculptures

2004

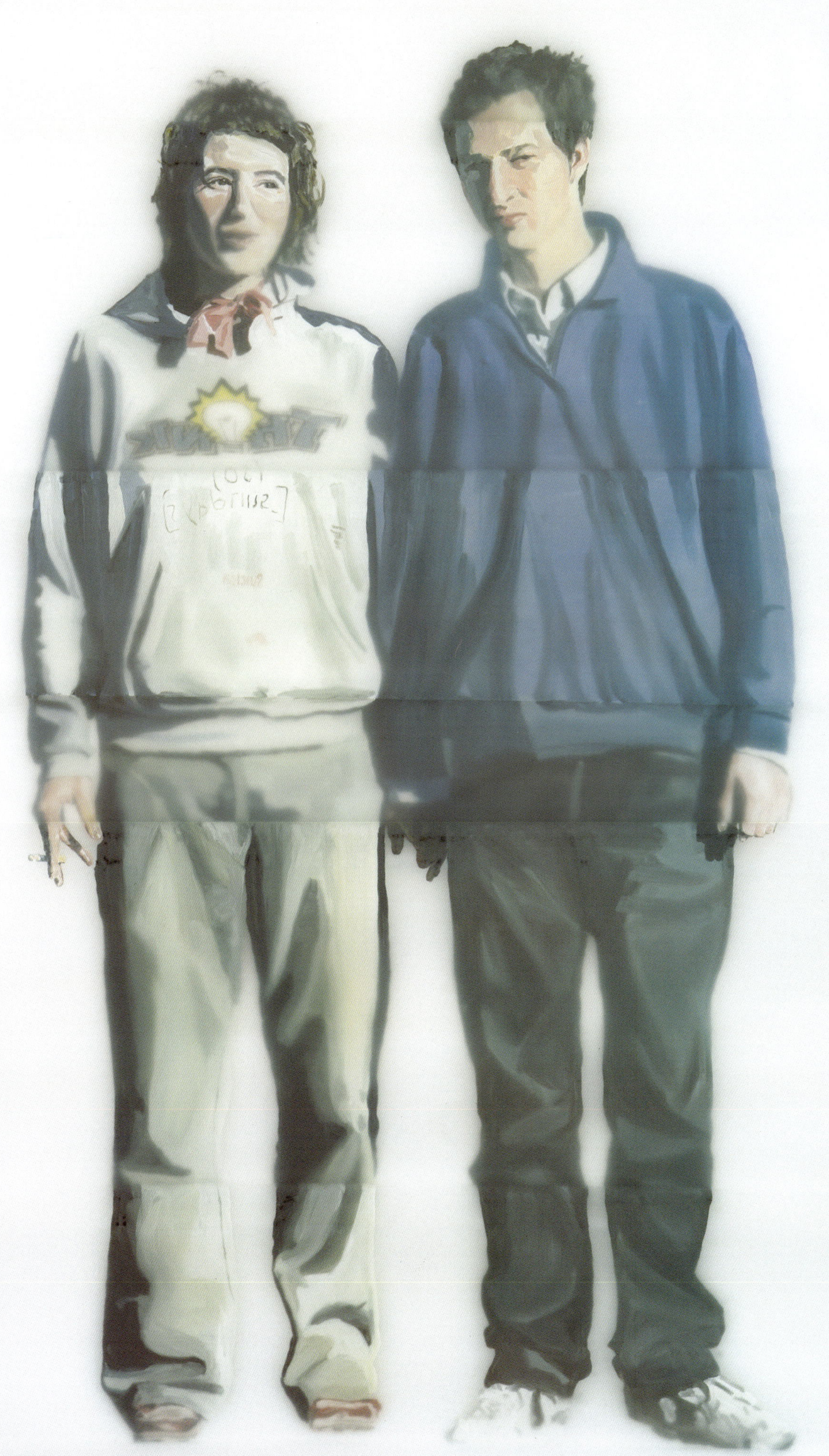

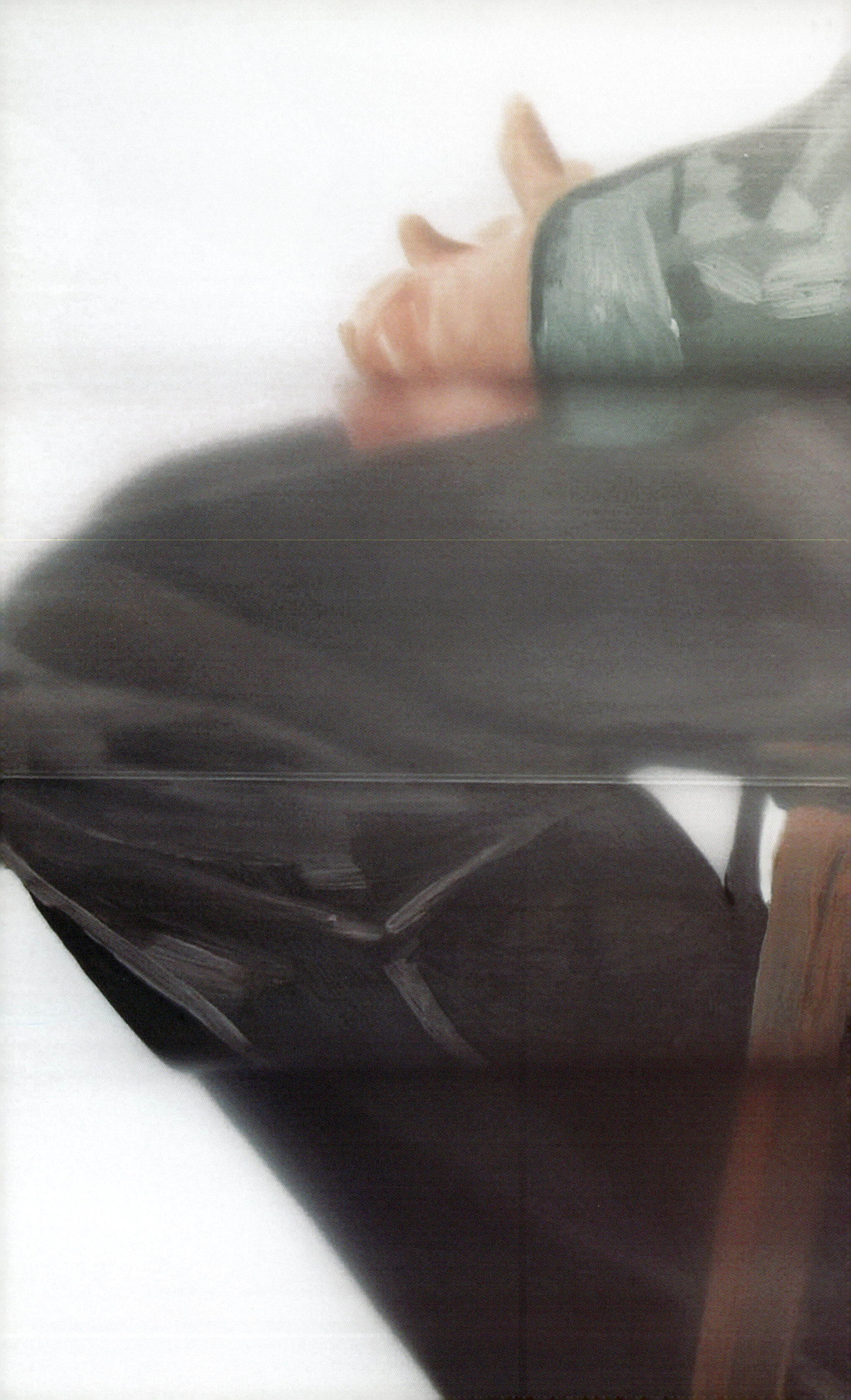

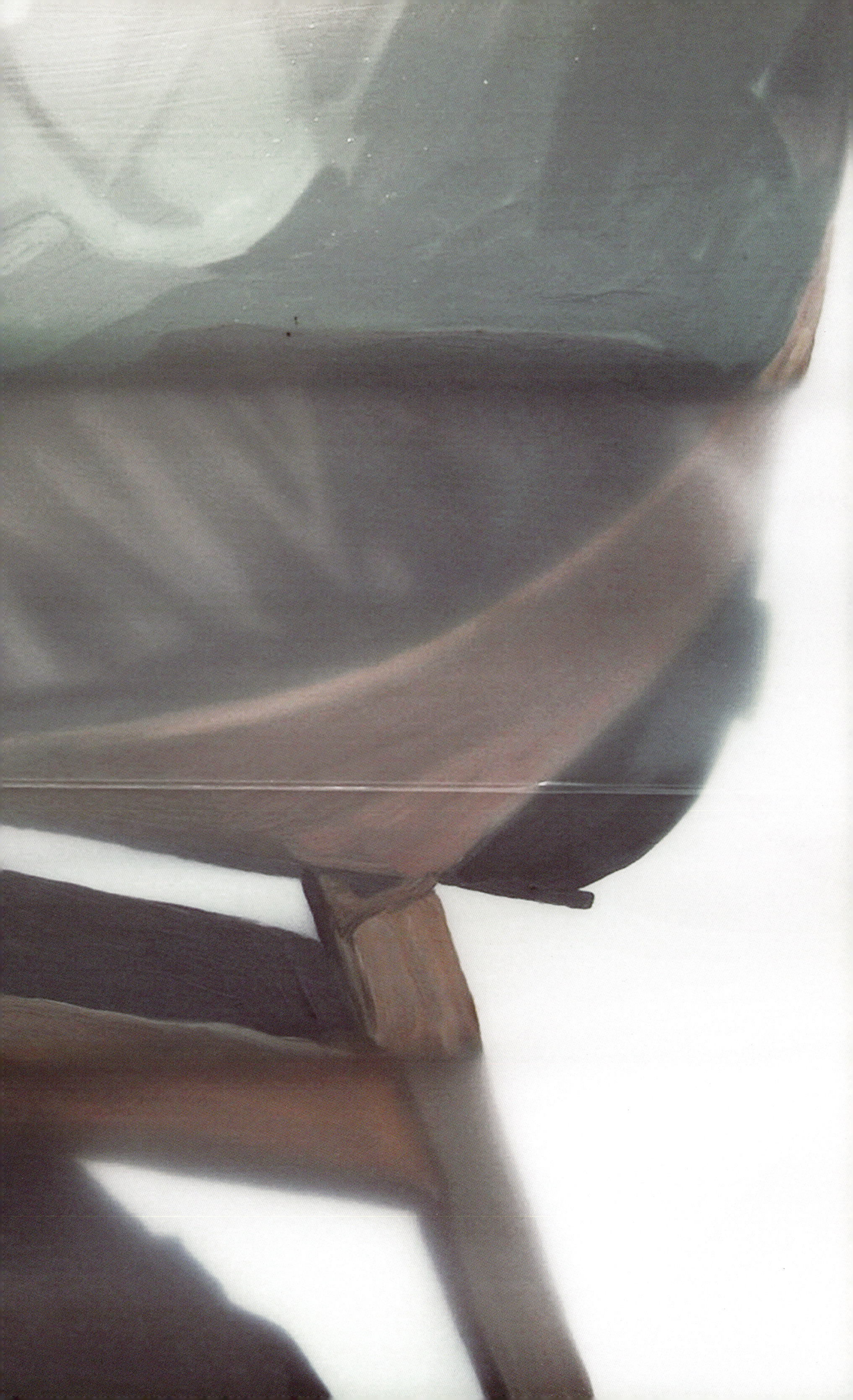

10

Erwin

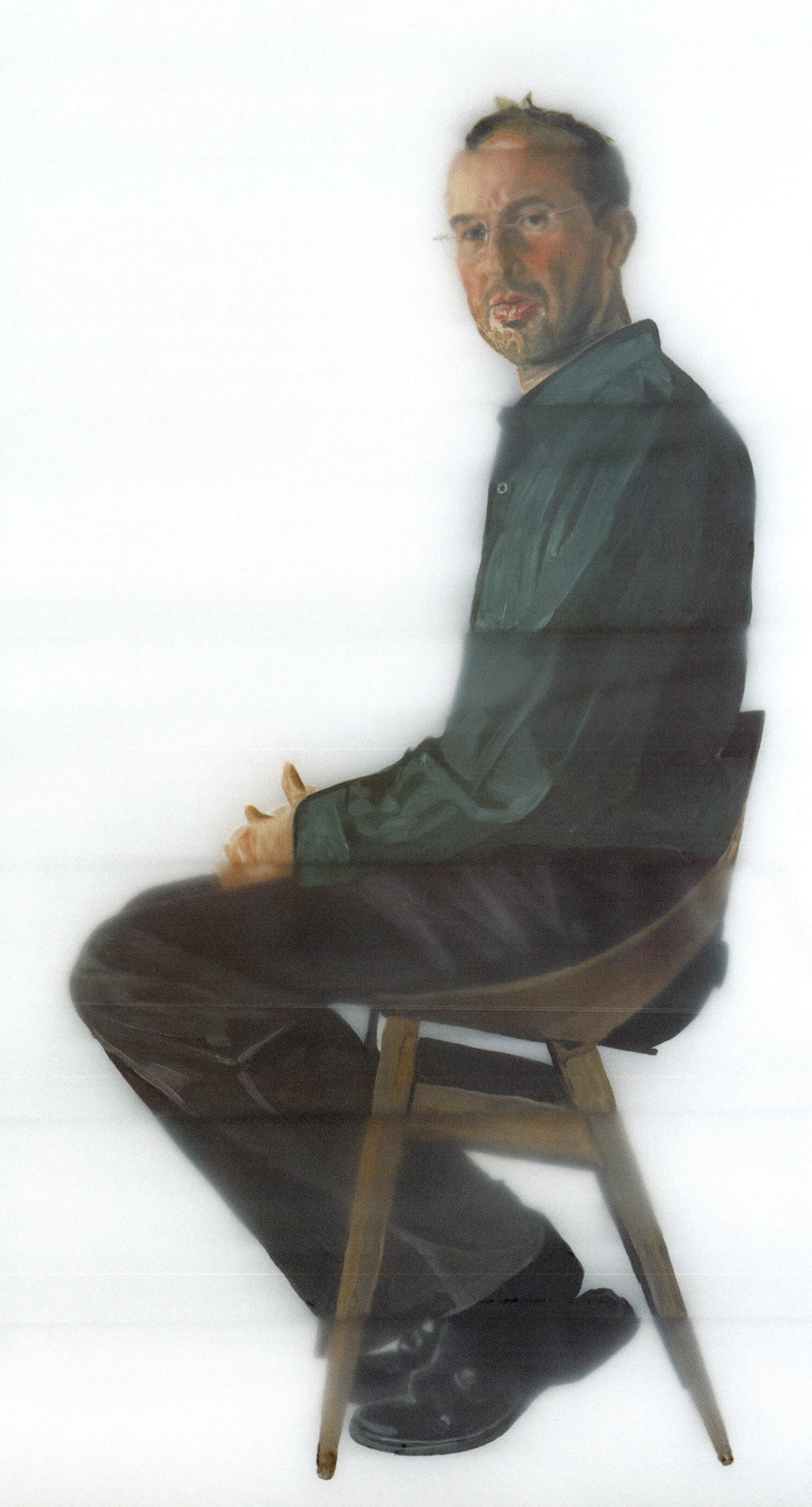

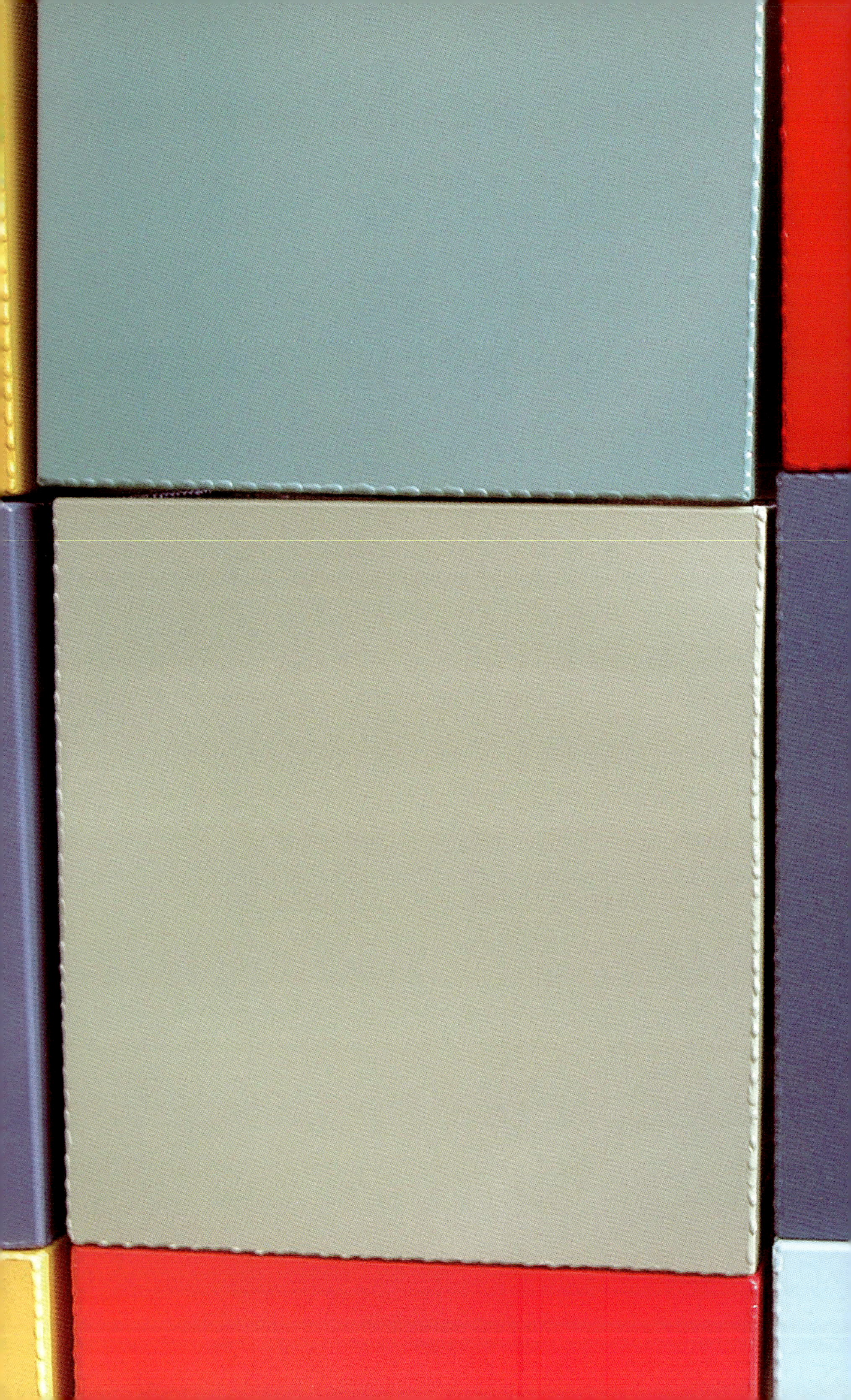

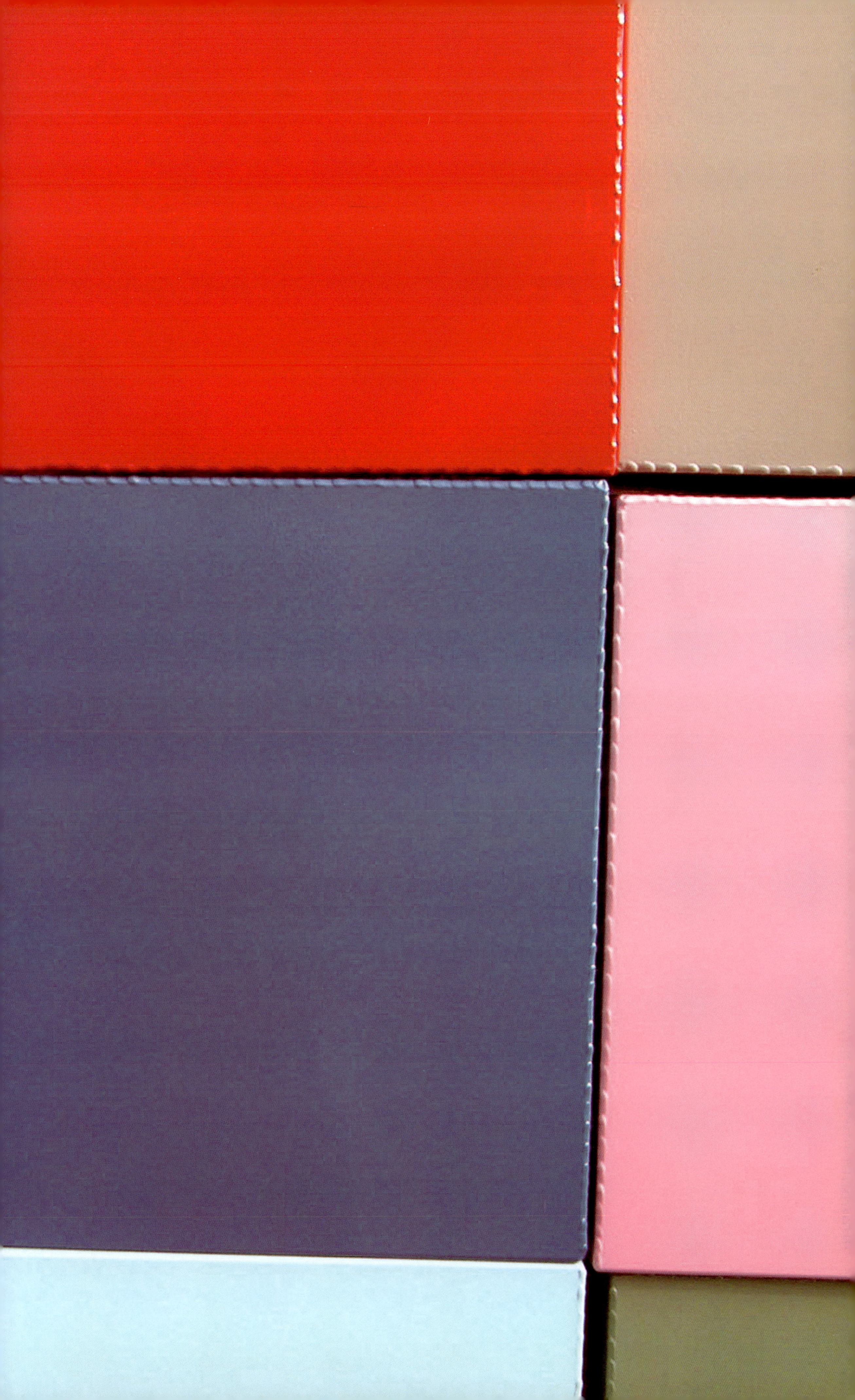

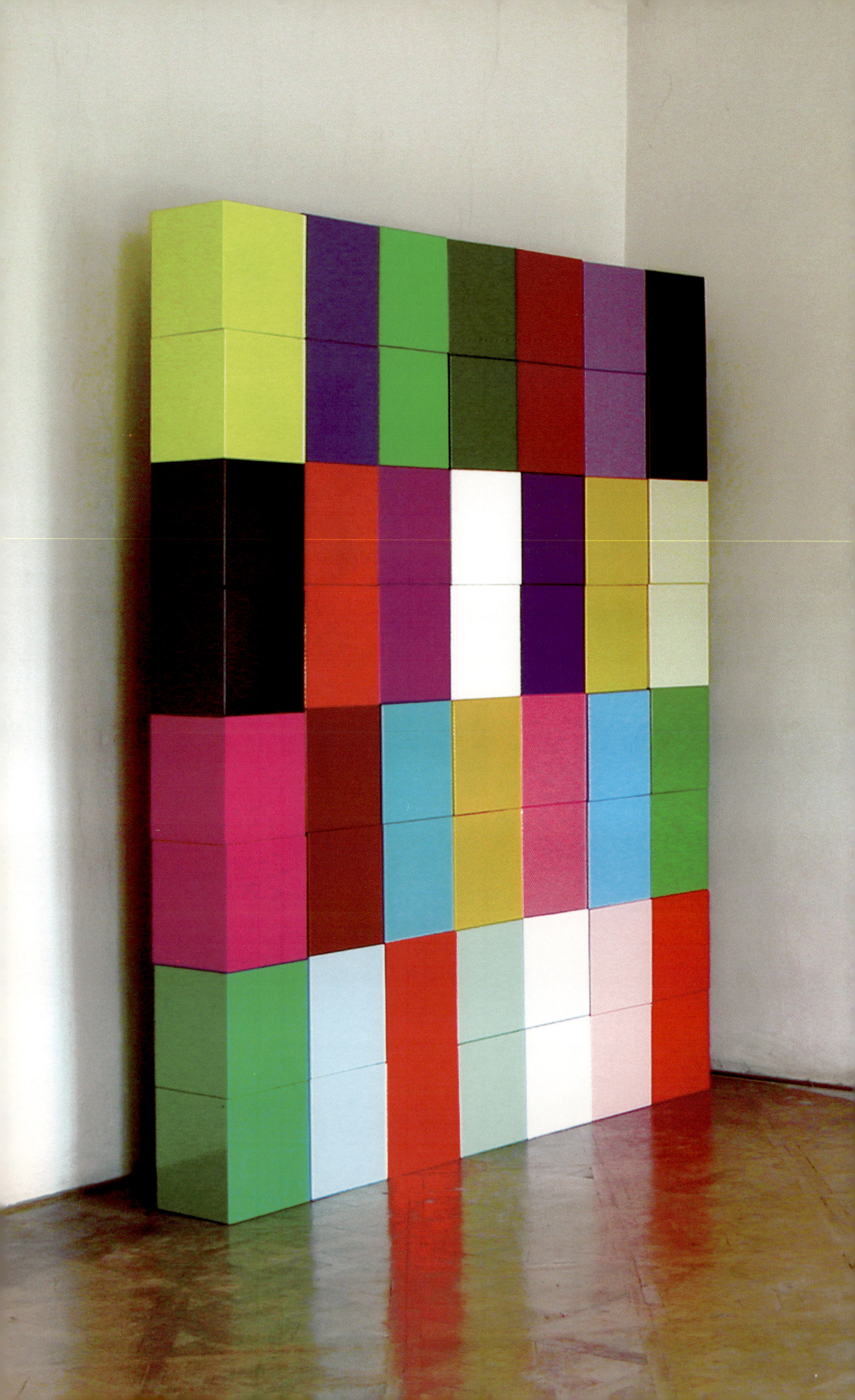

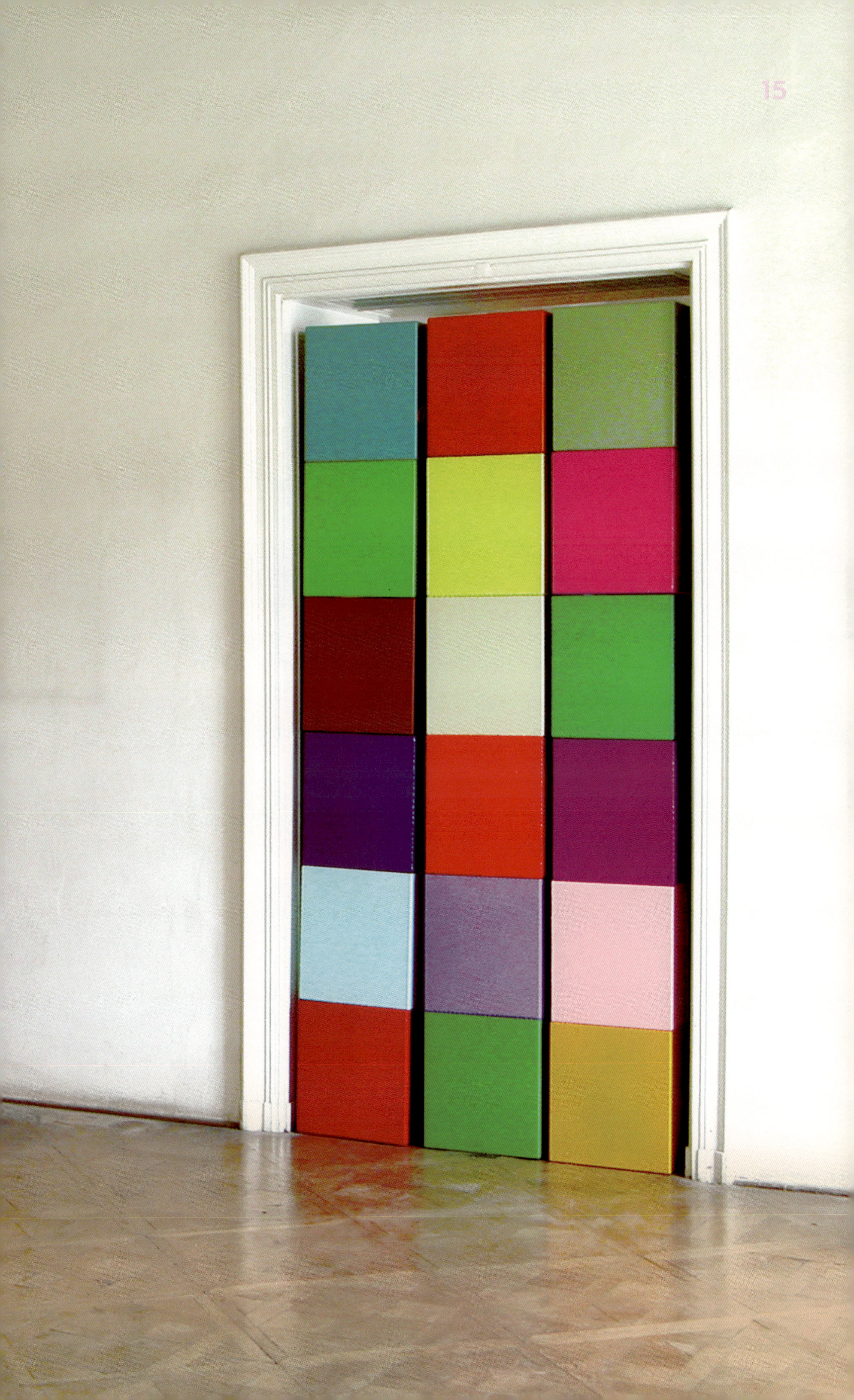

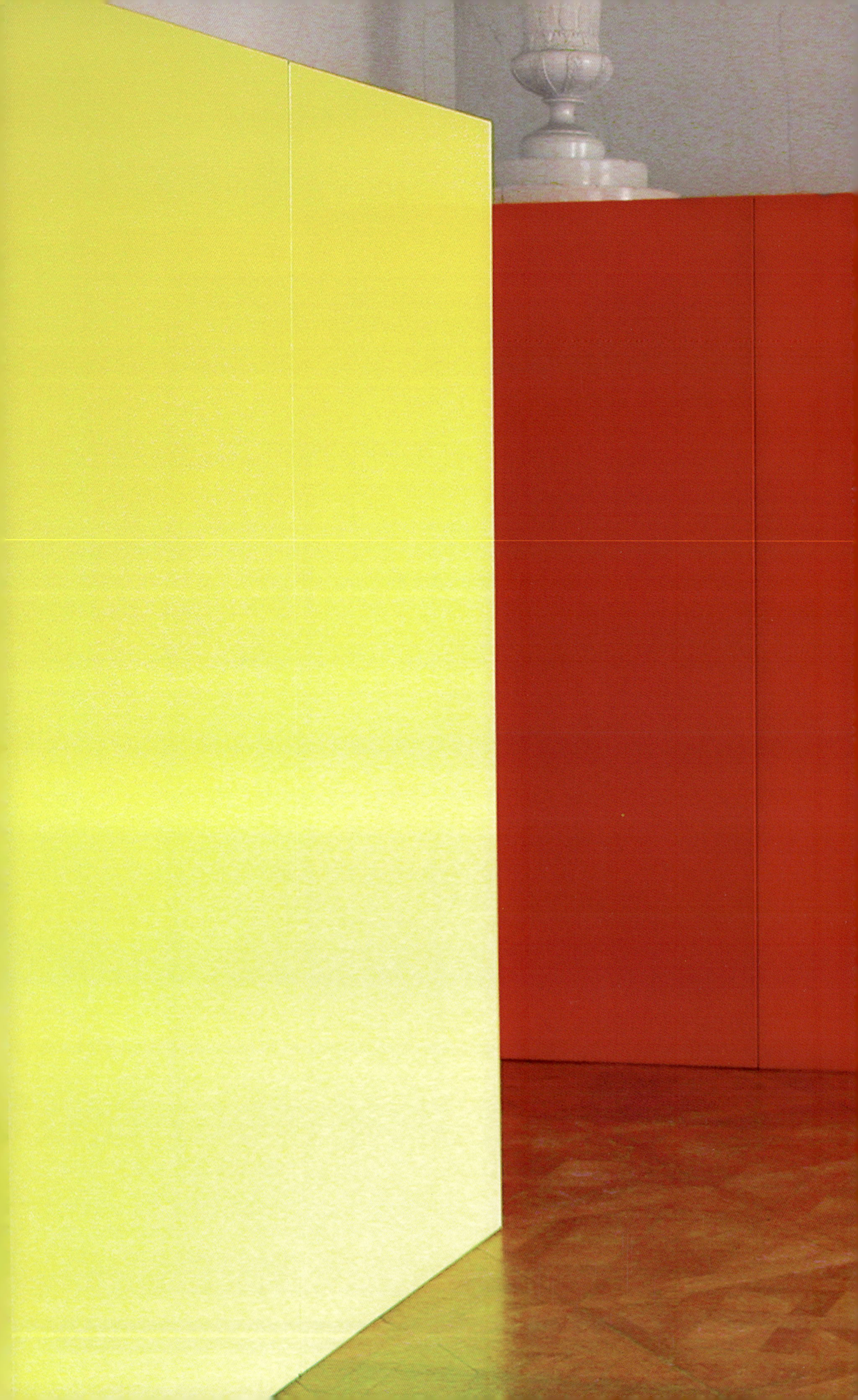

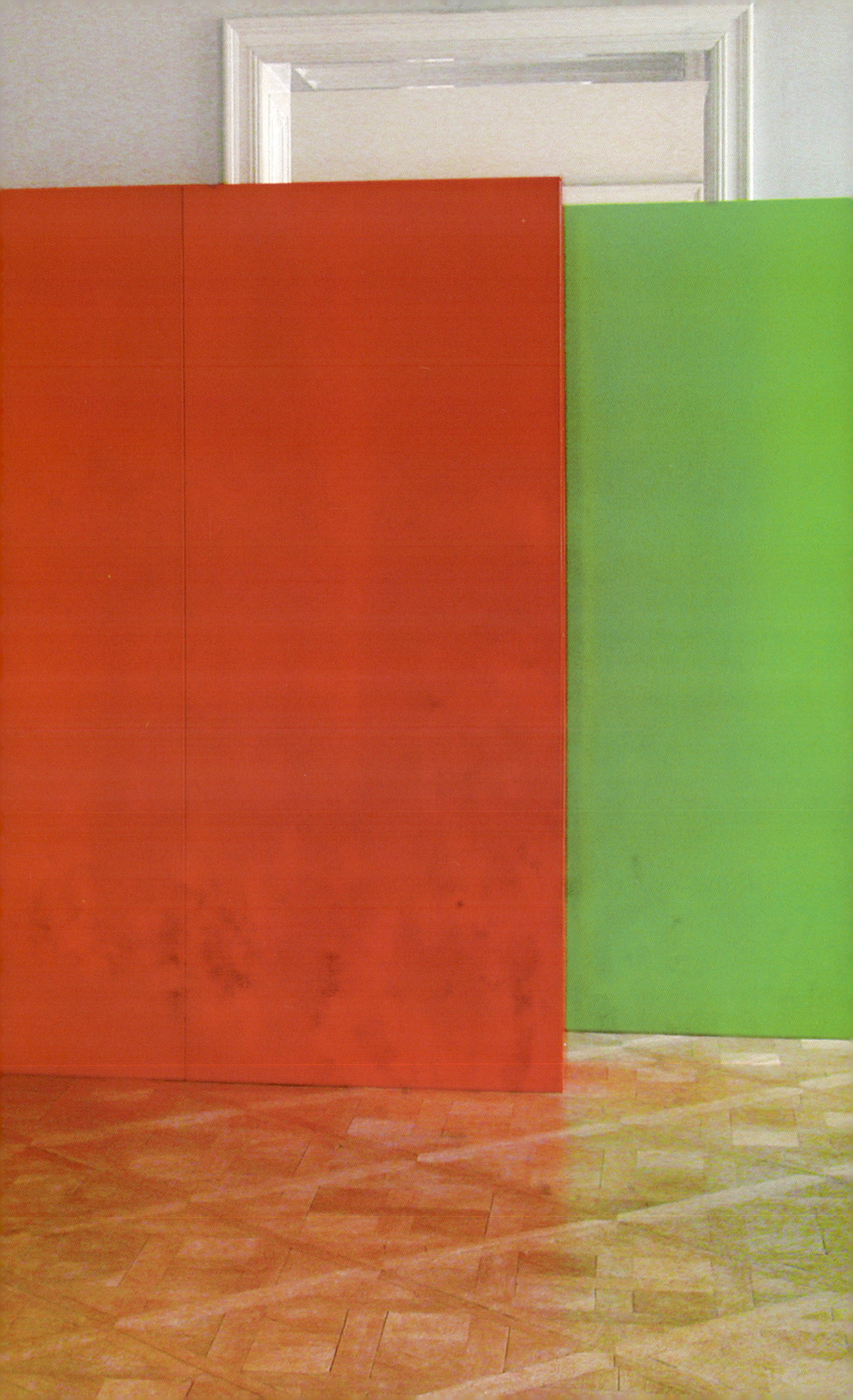

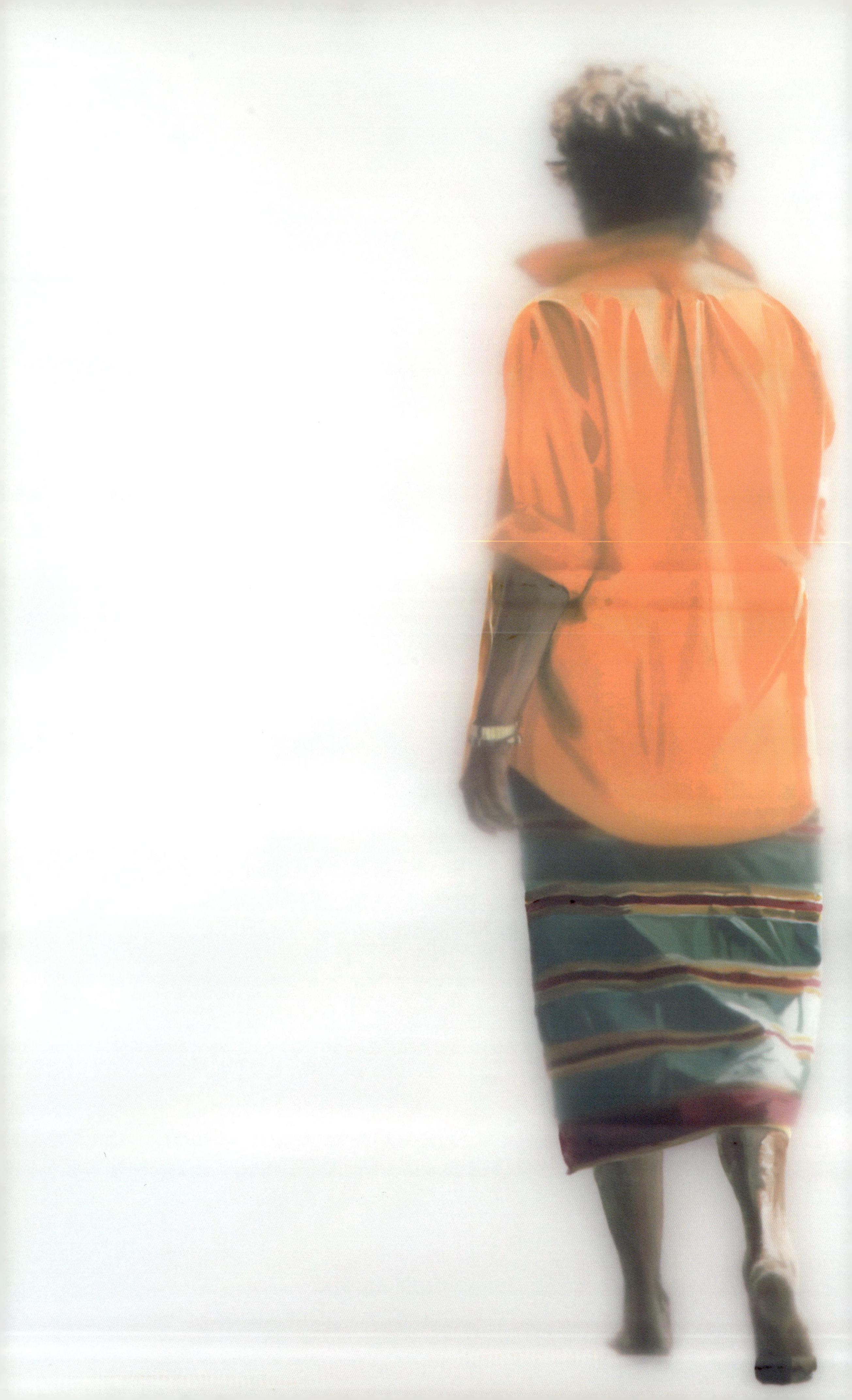

Christl

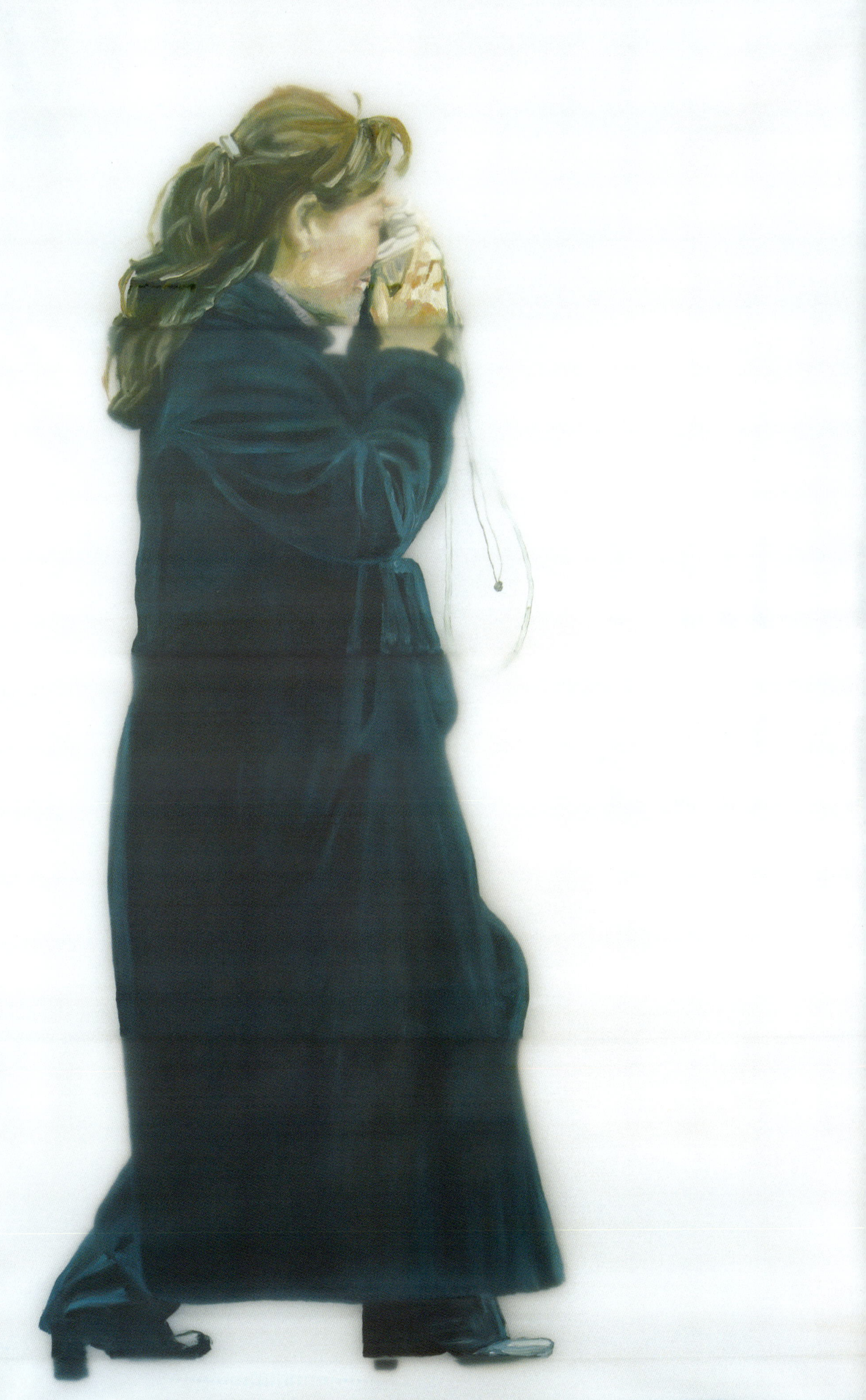

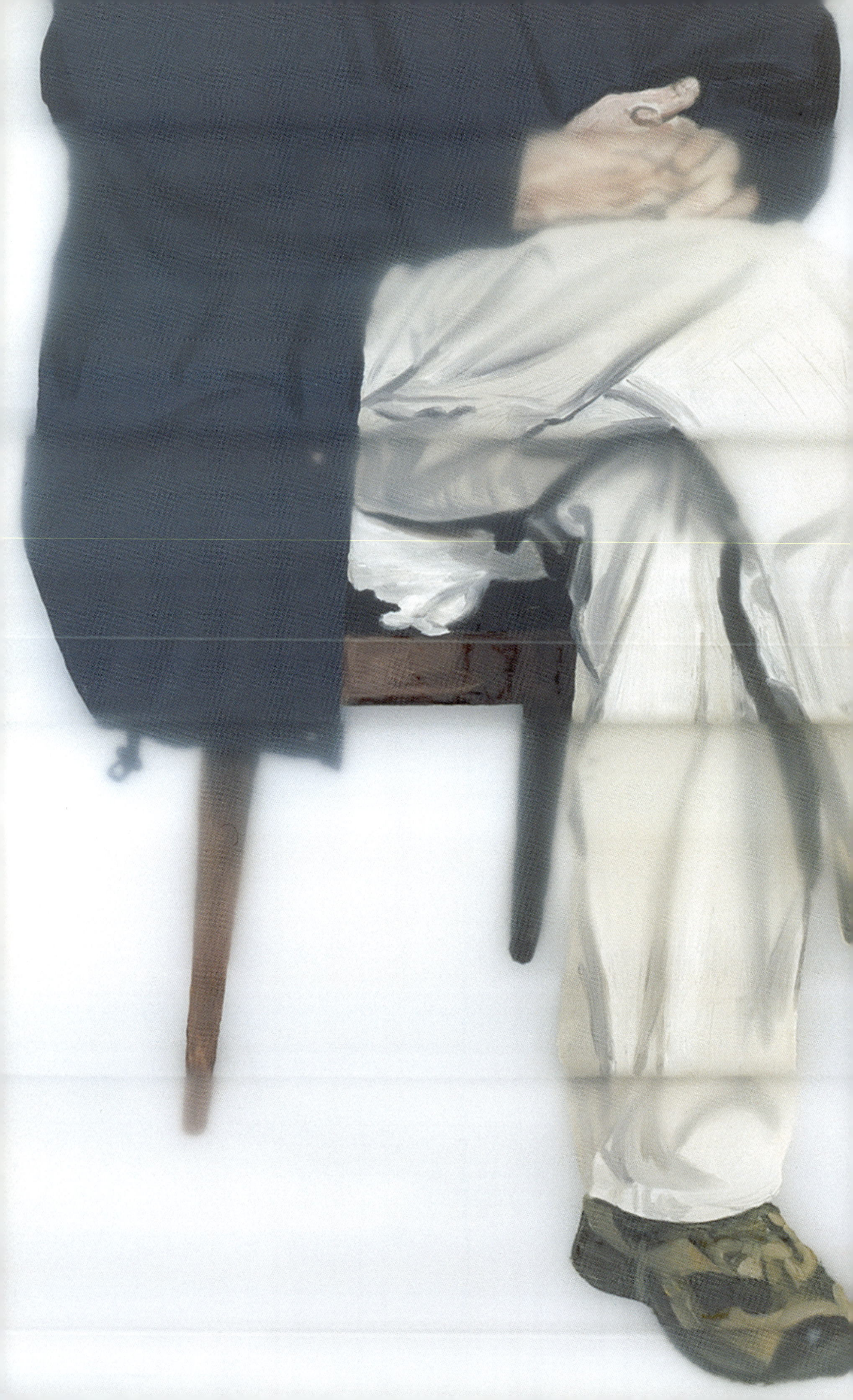

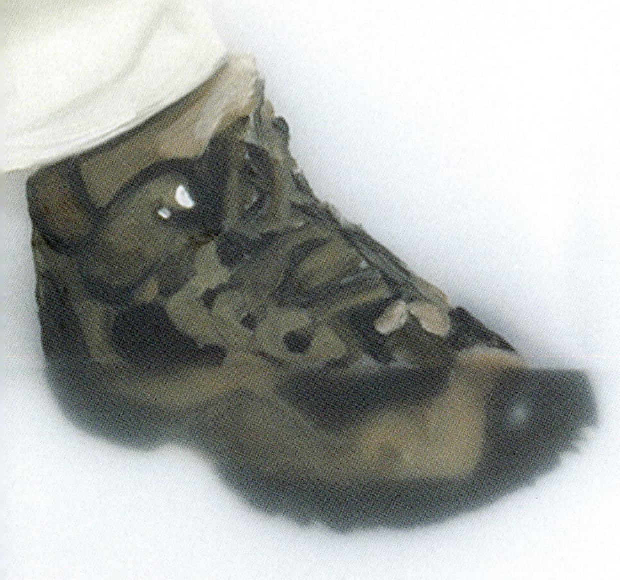

Christophe

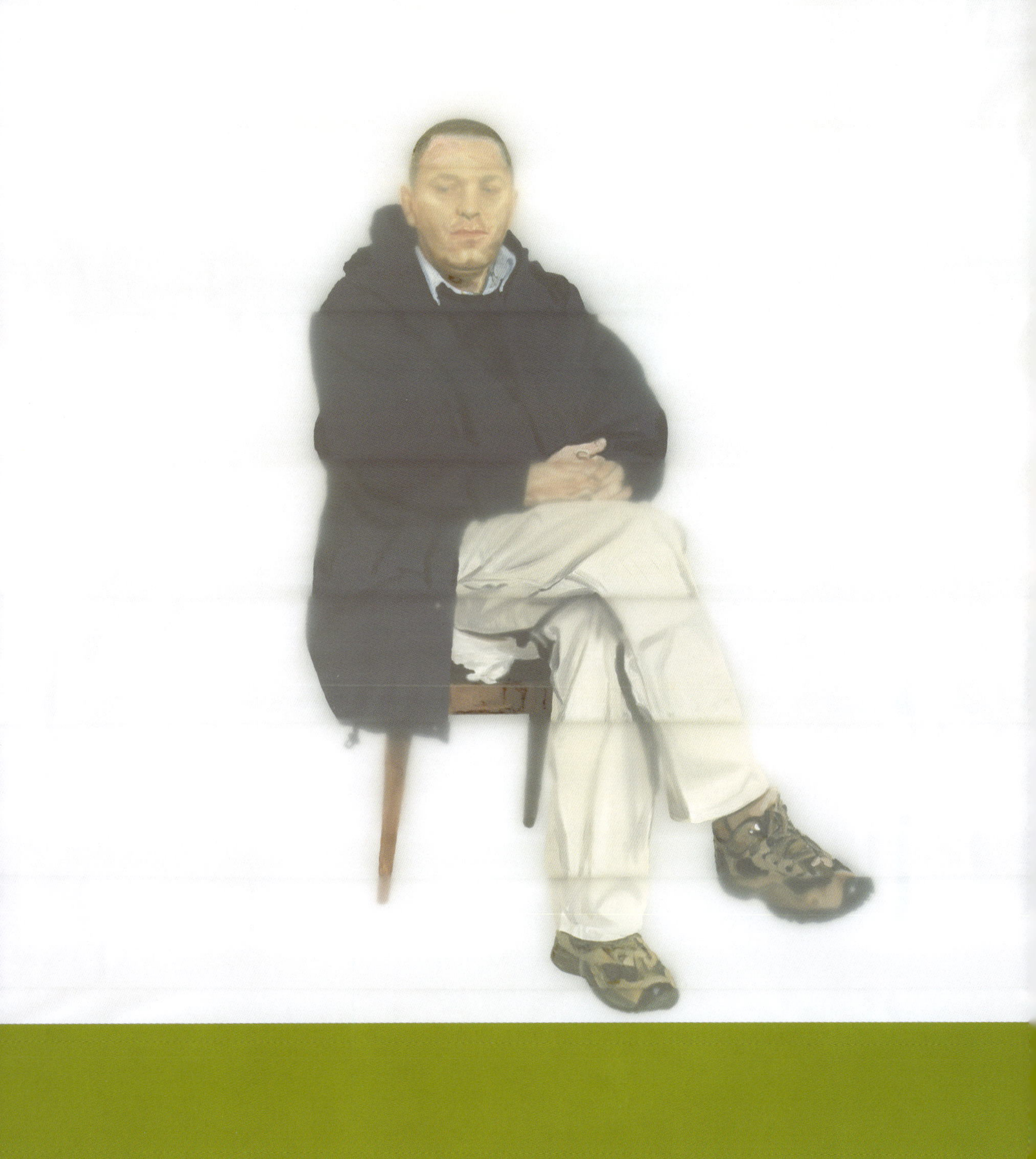

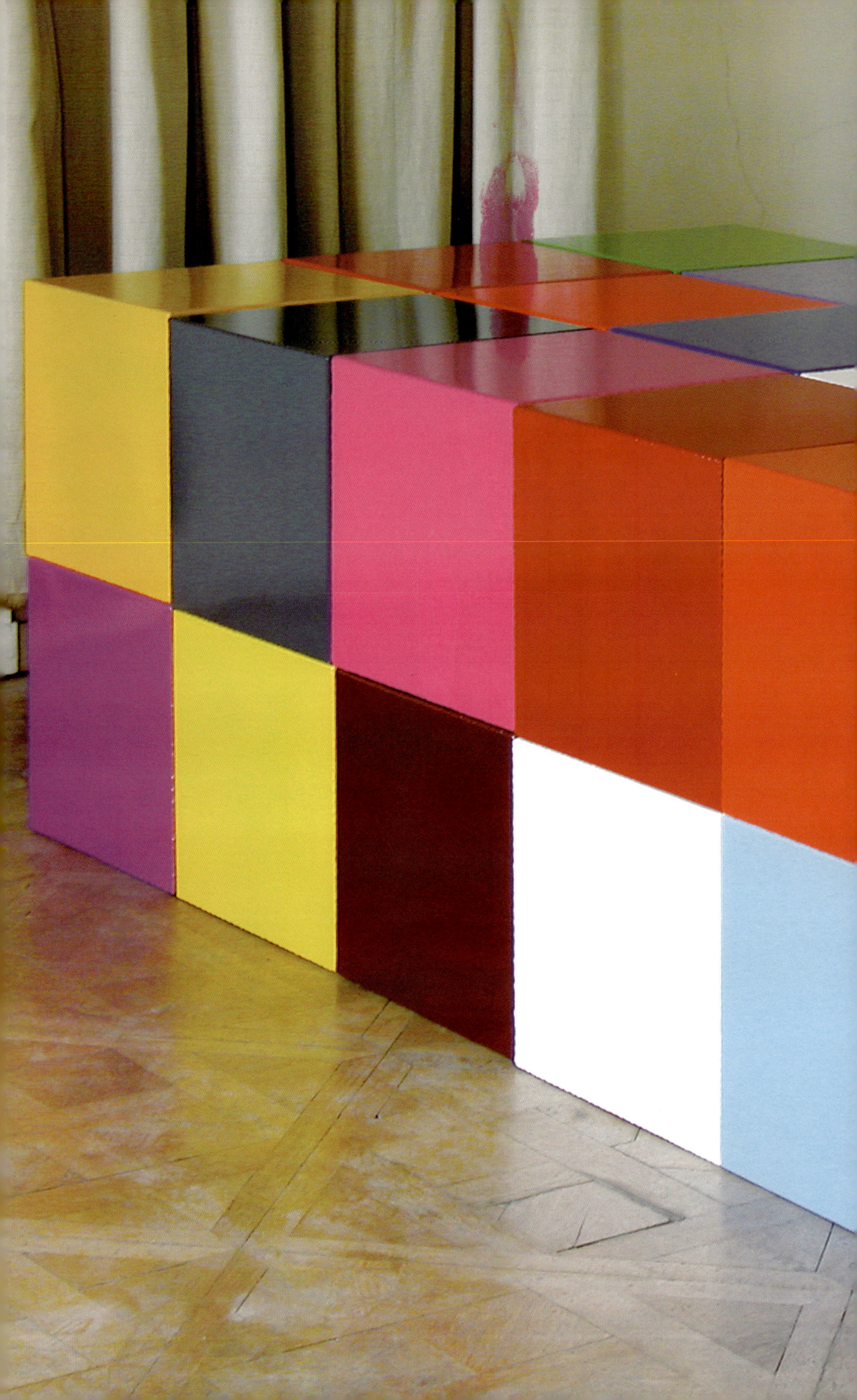

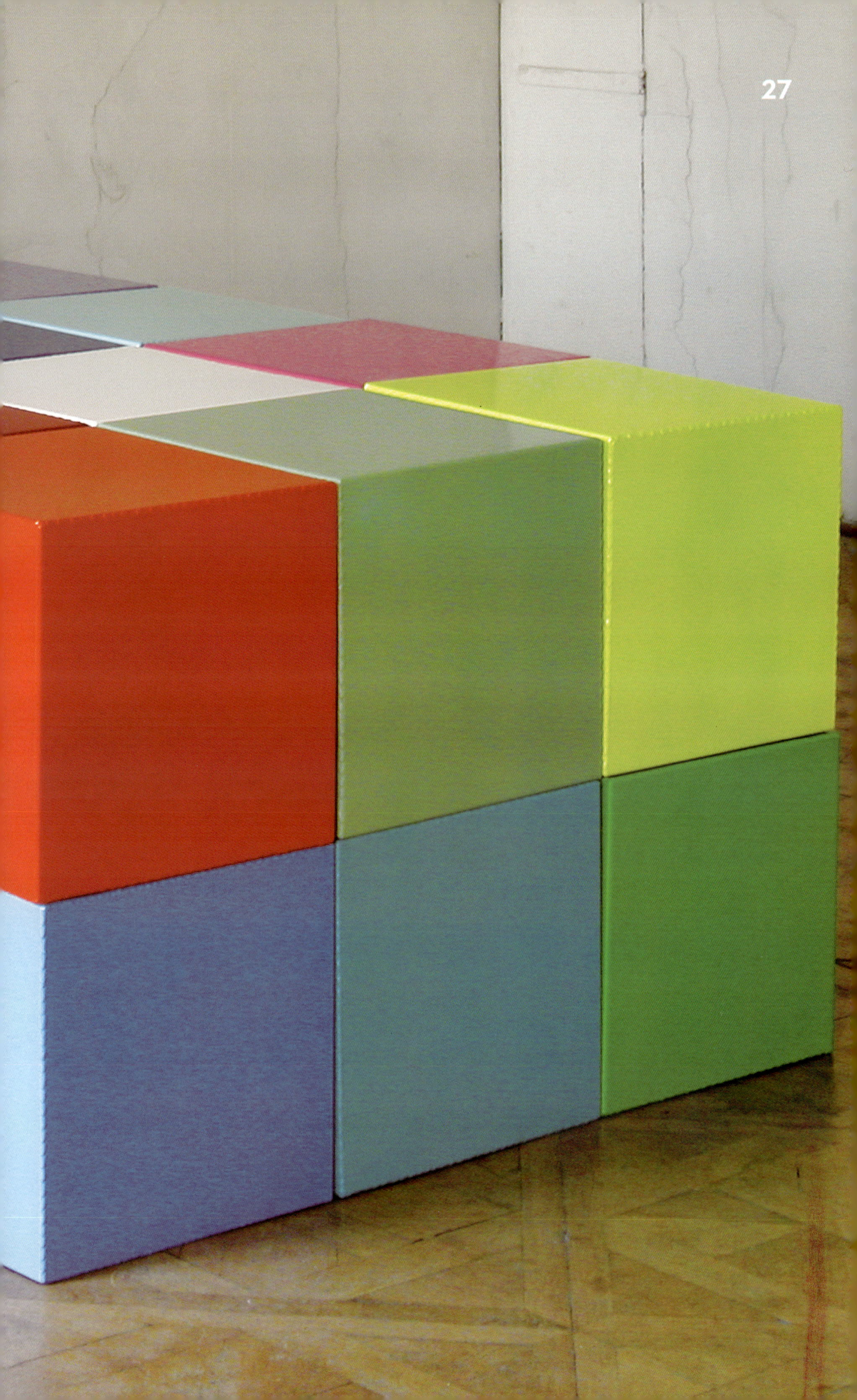

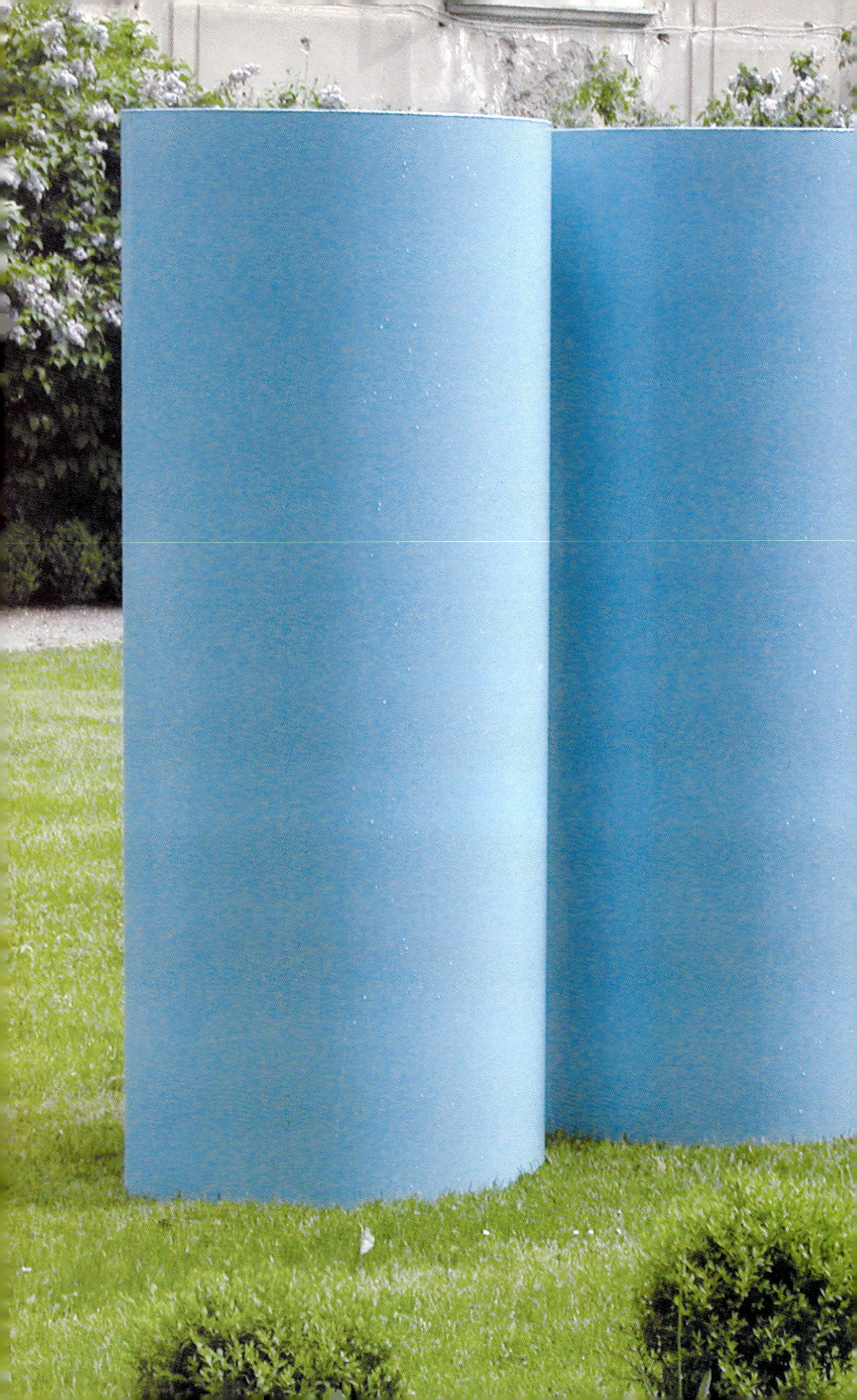

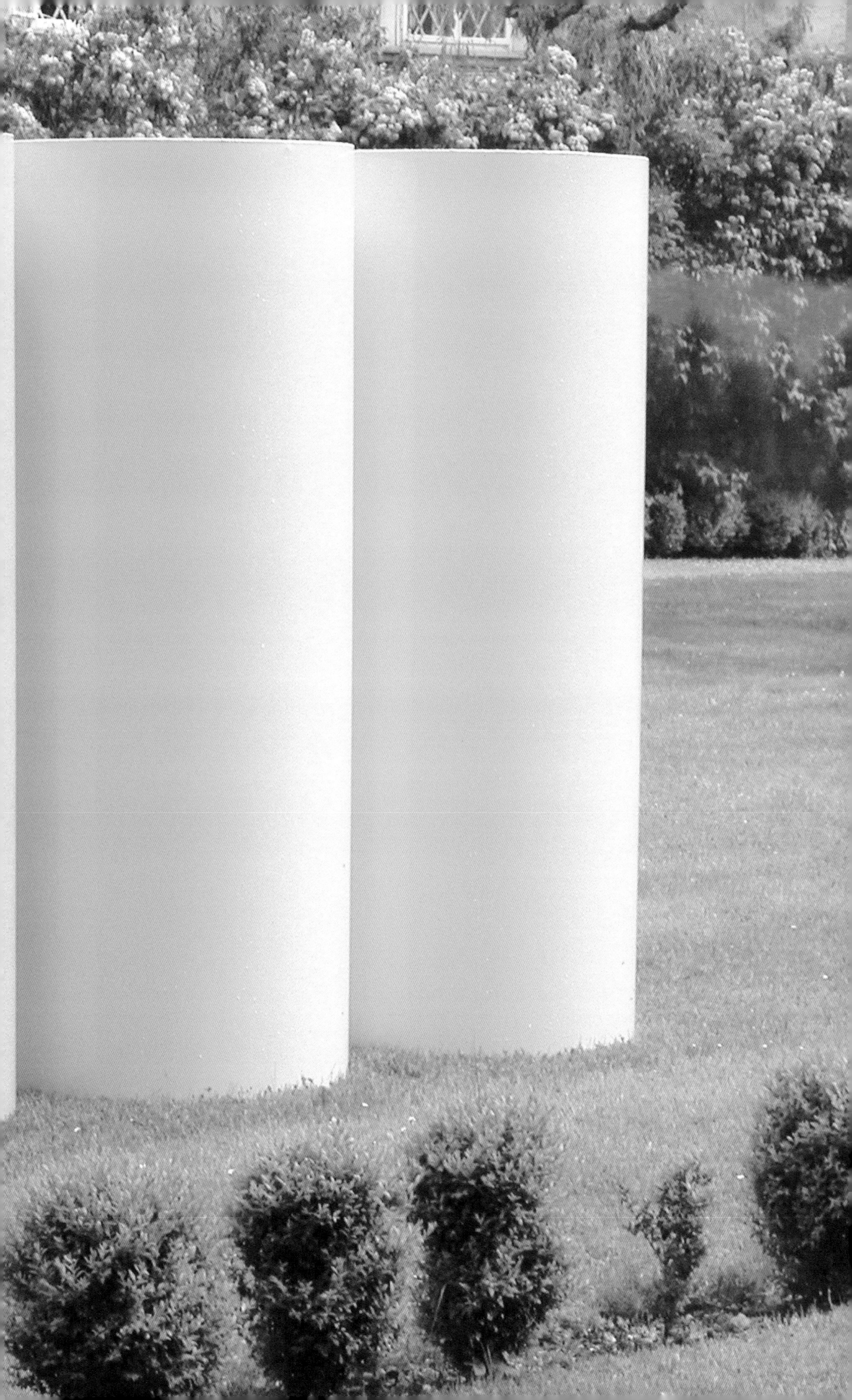

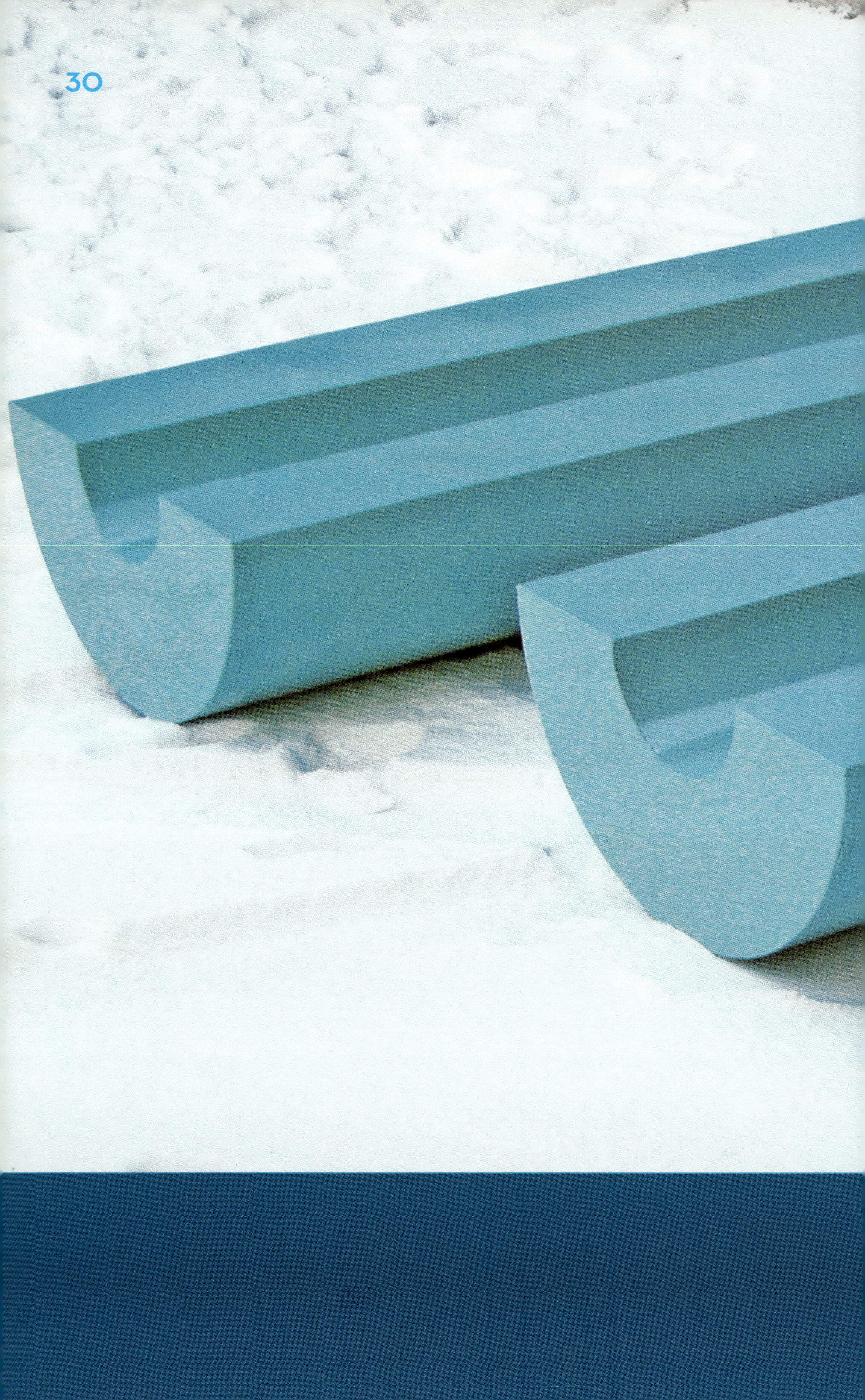

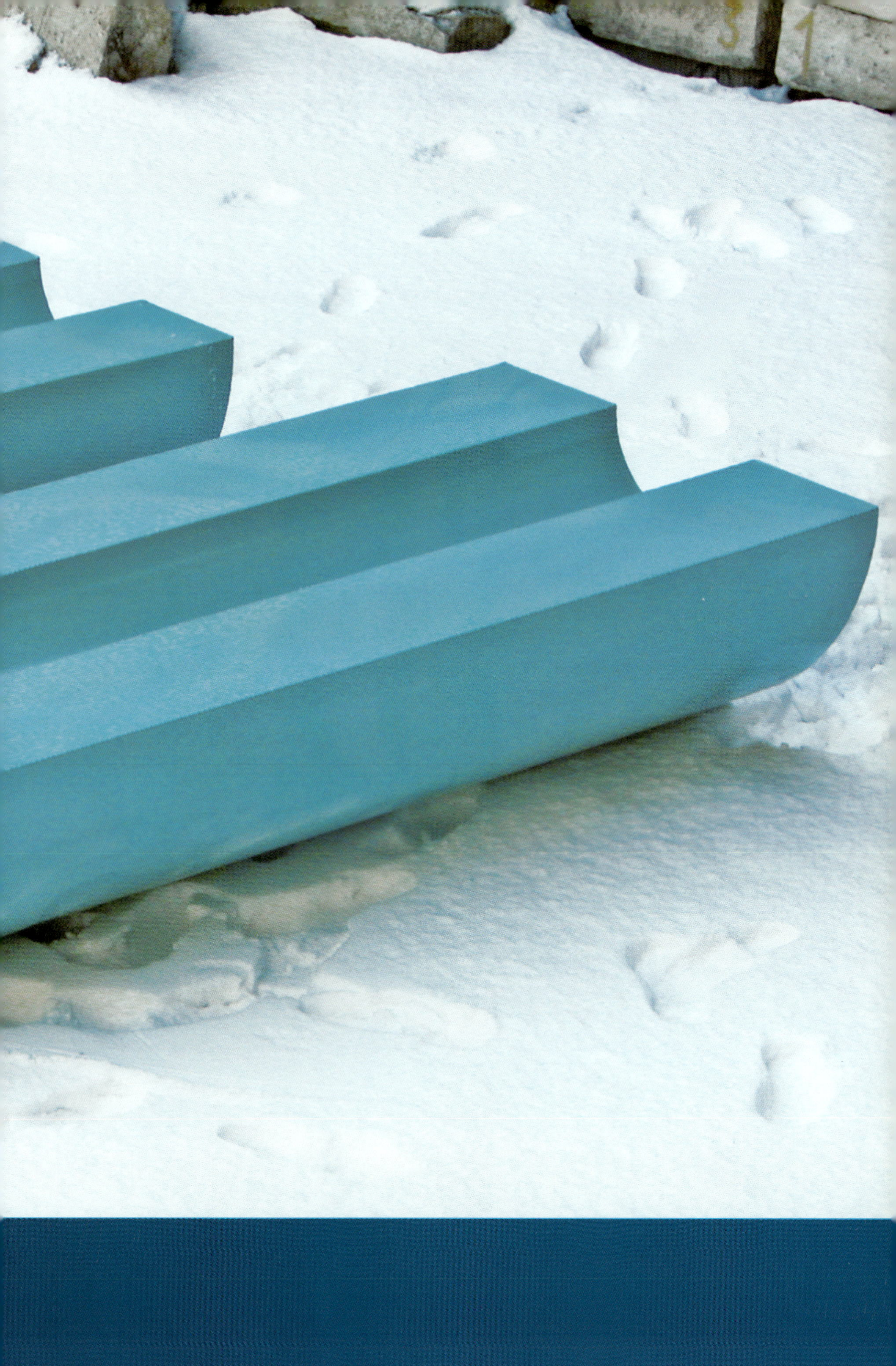

Alix

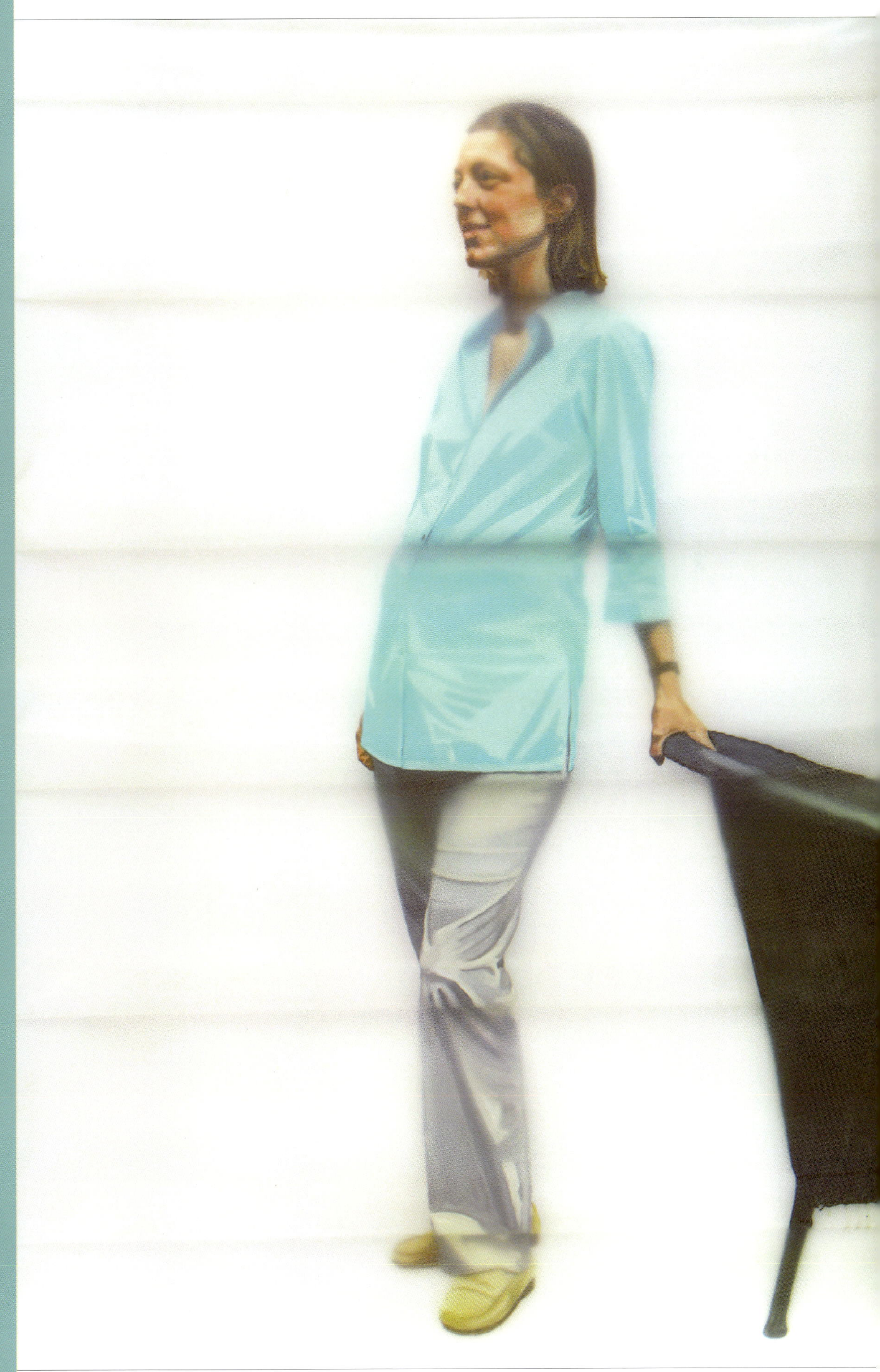

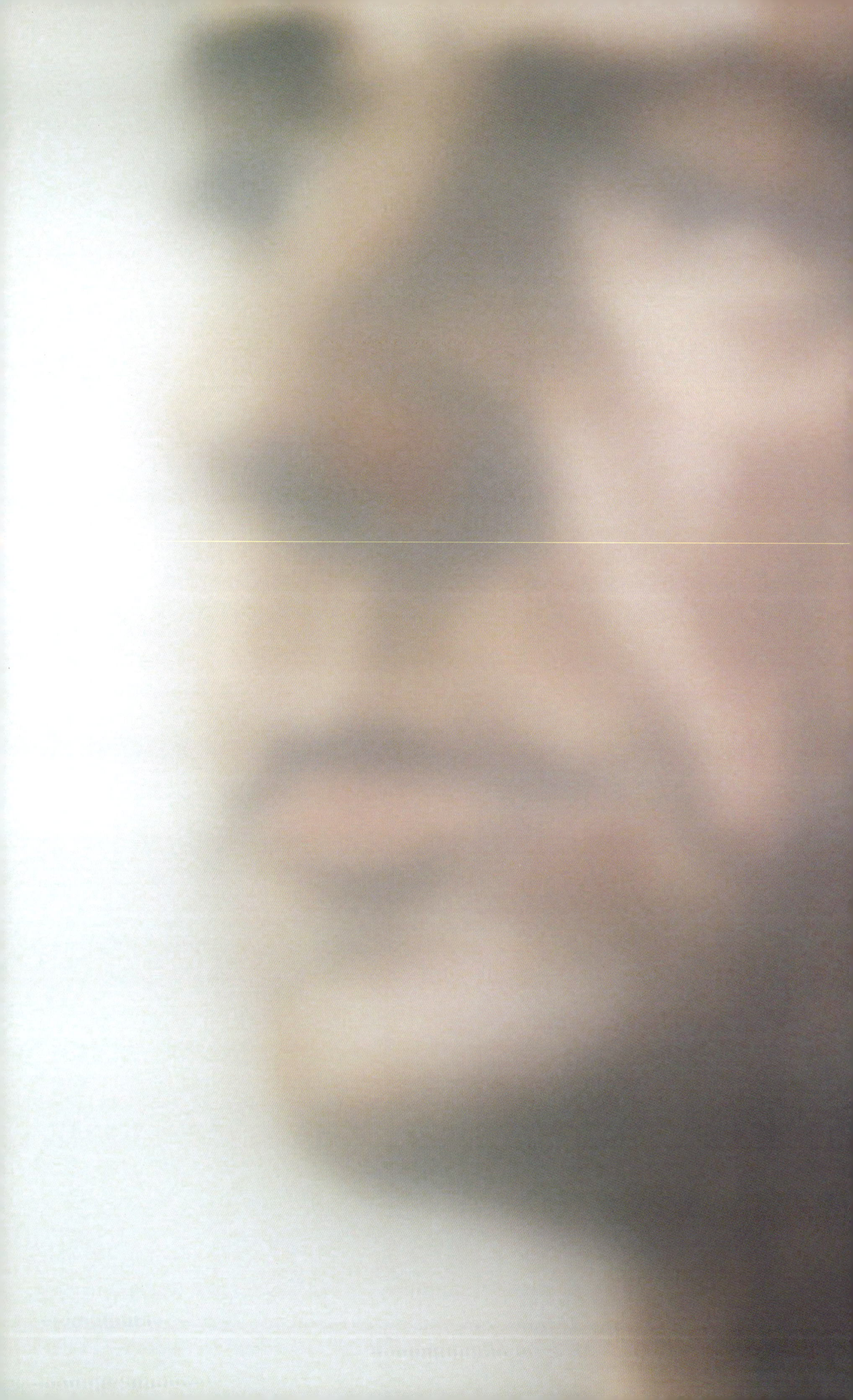

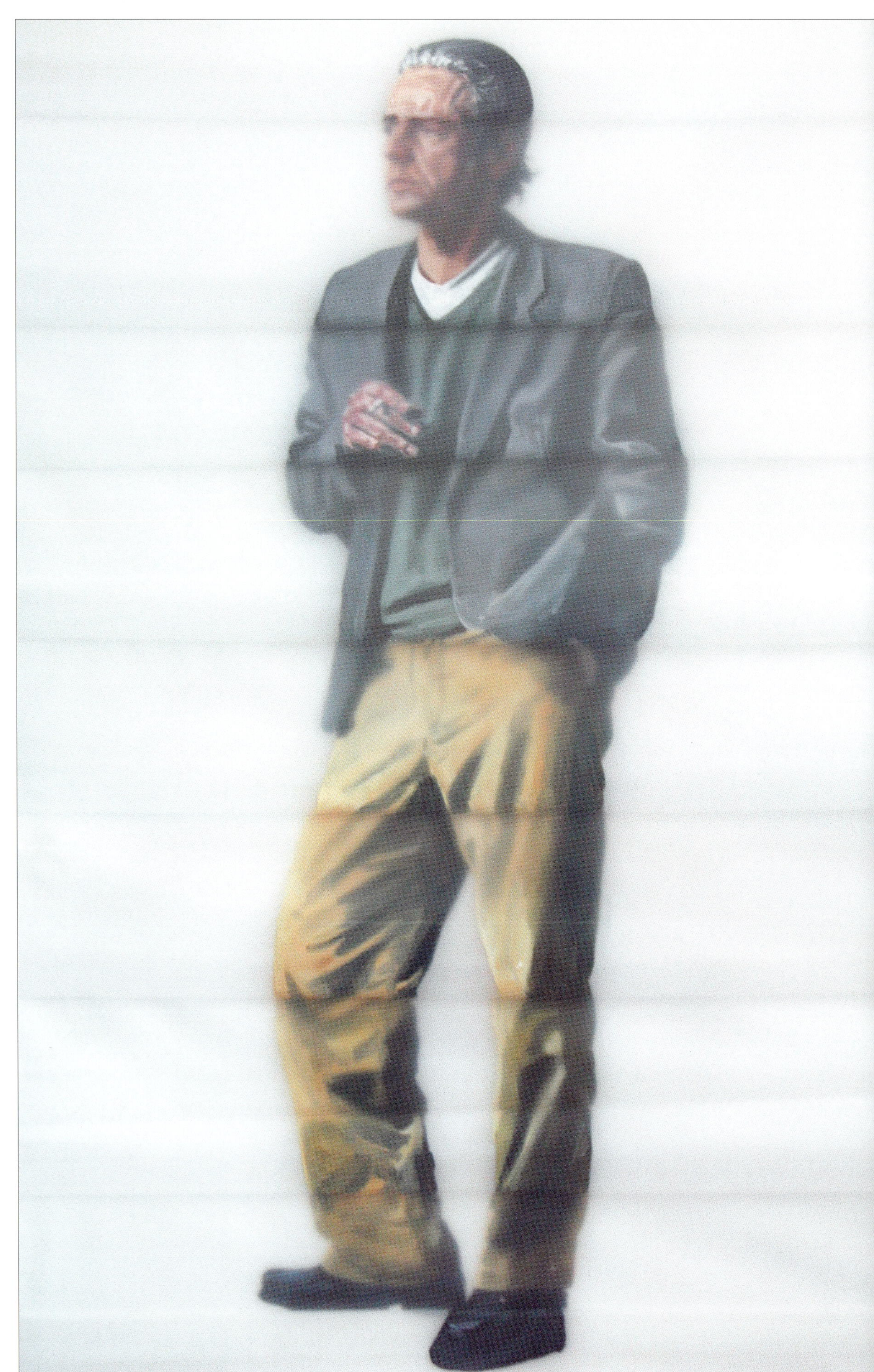

Rudolf

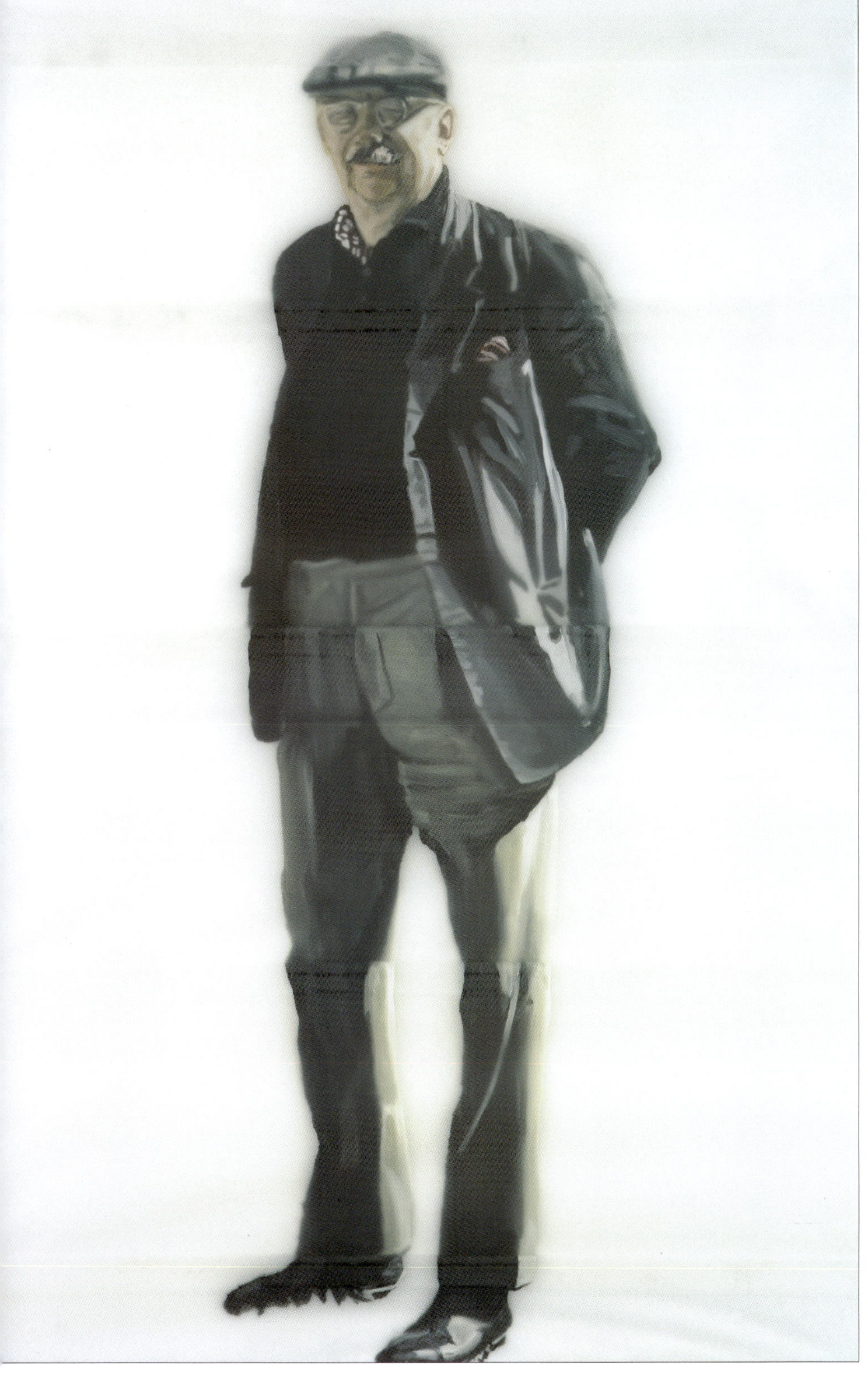

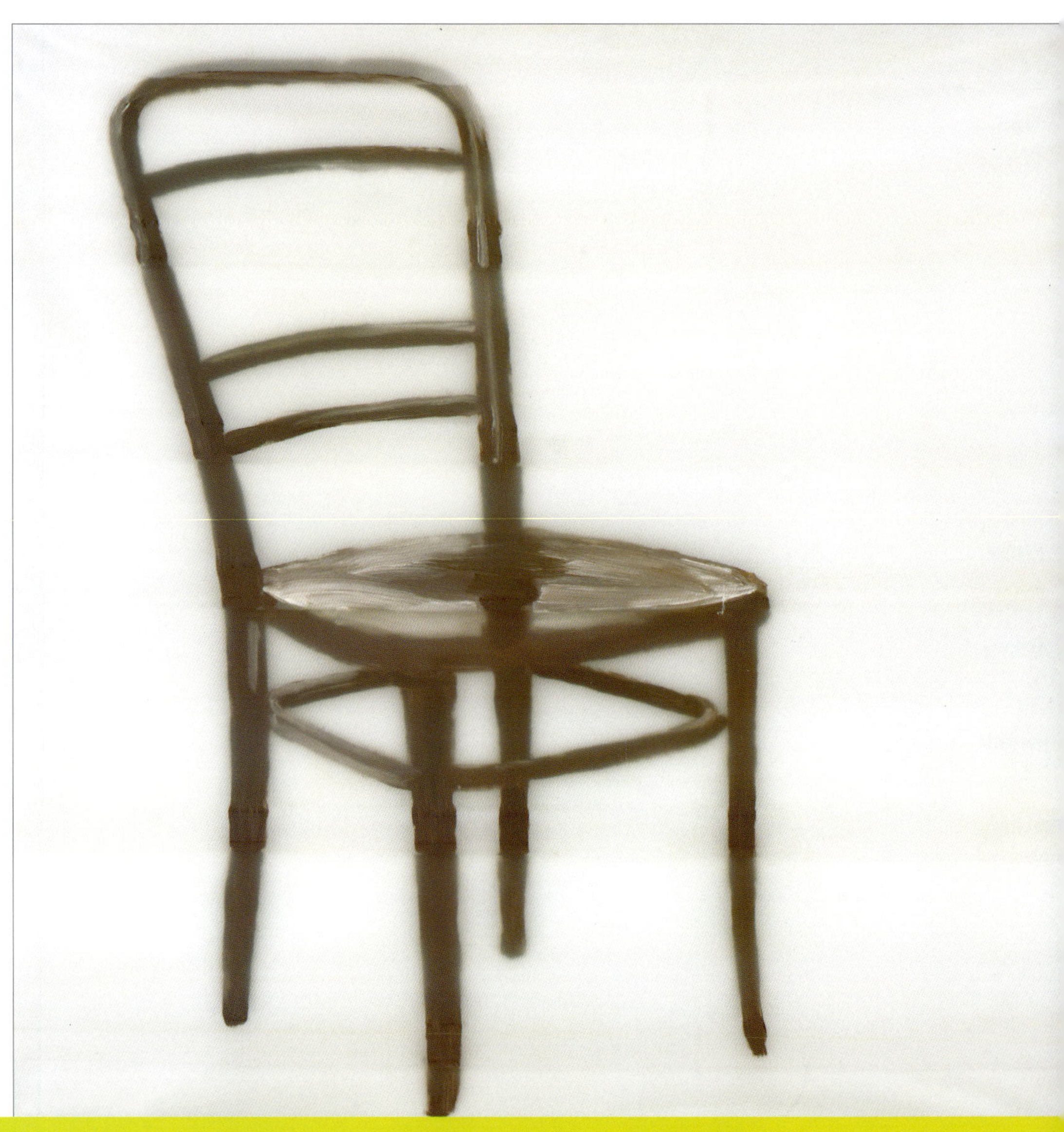

Chair 1

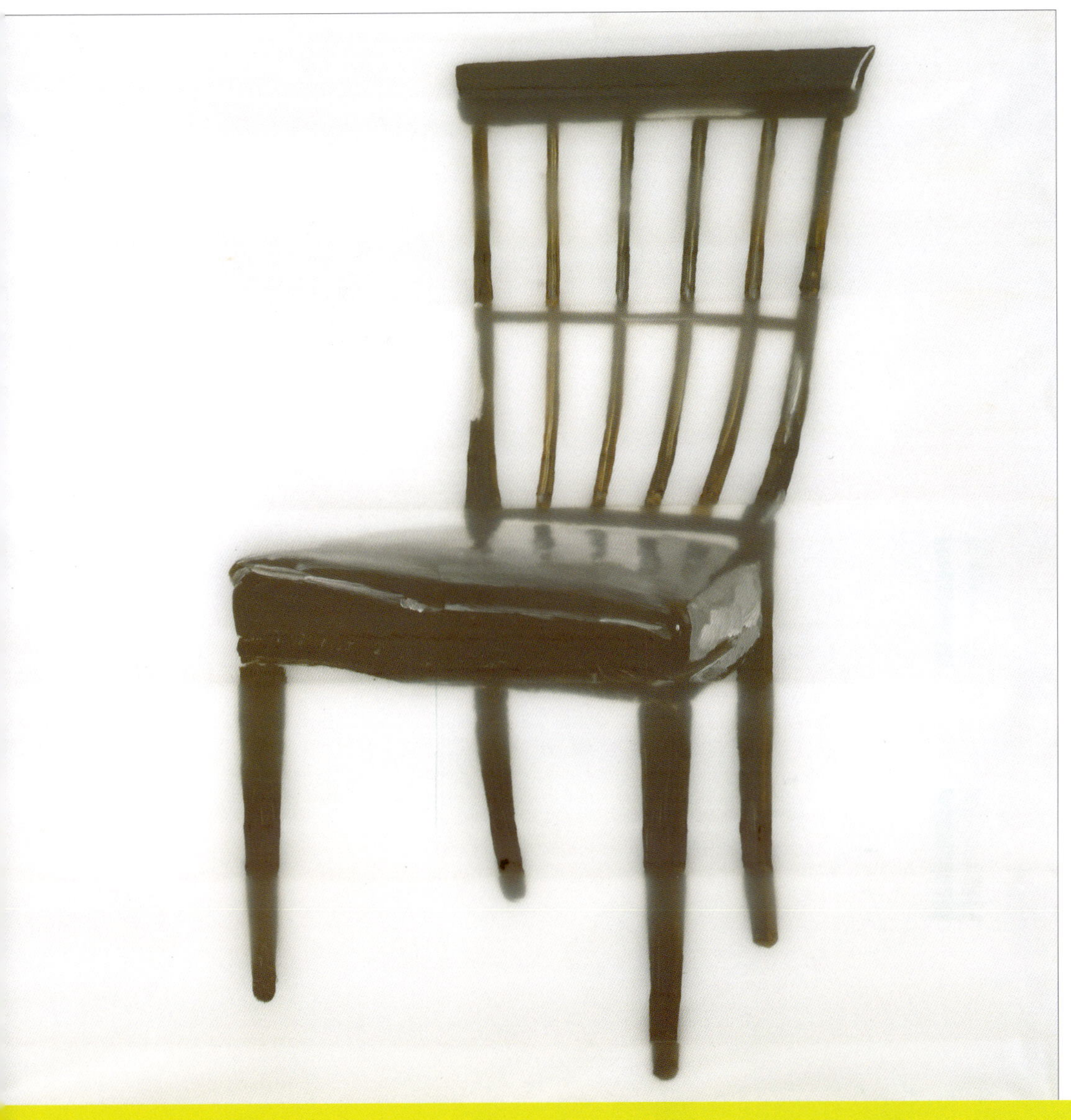

Chair 2

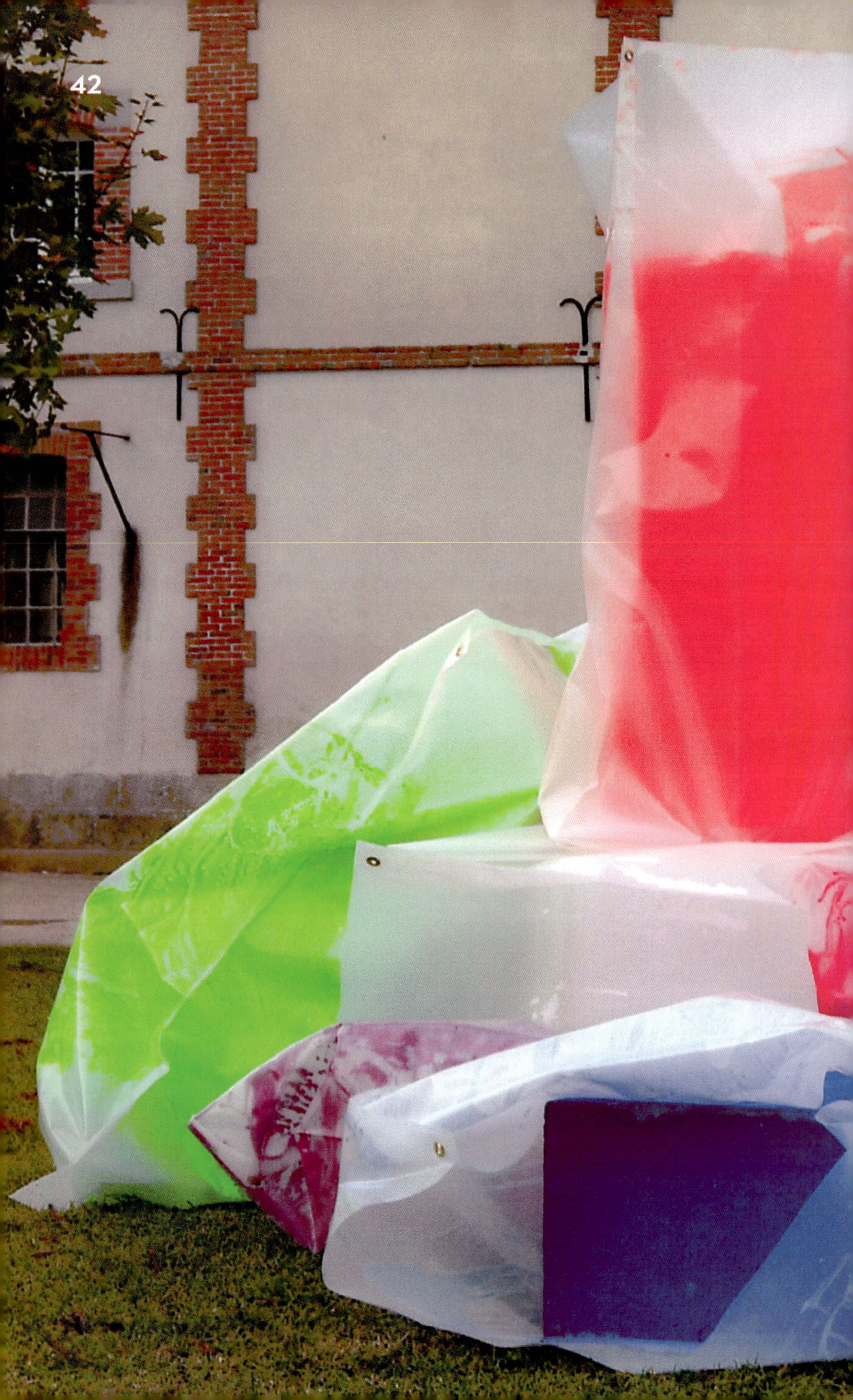

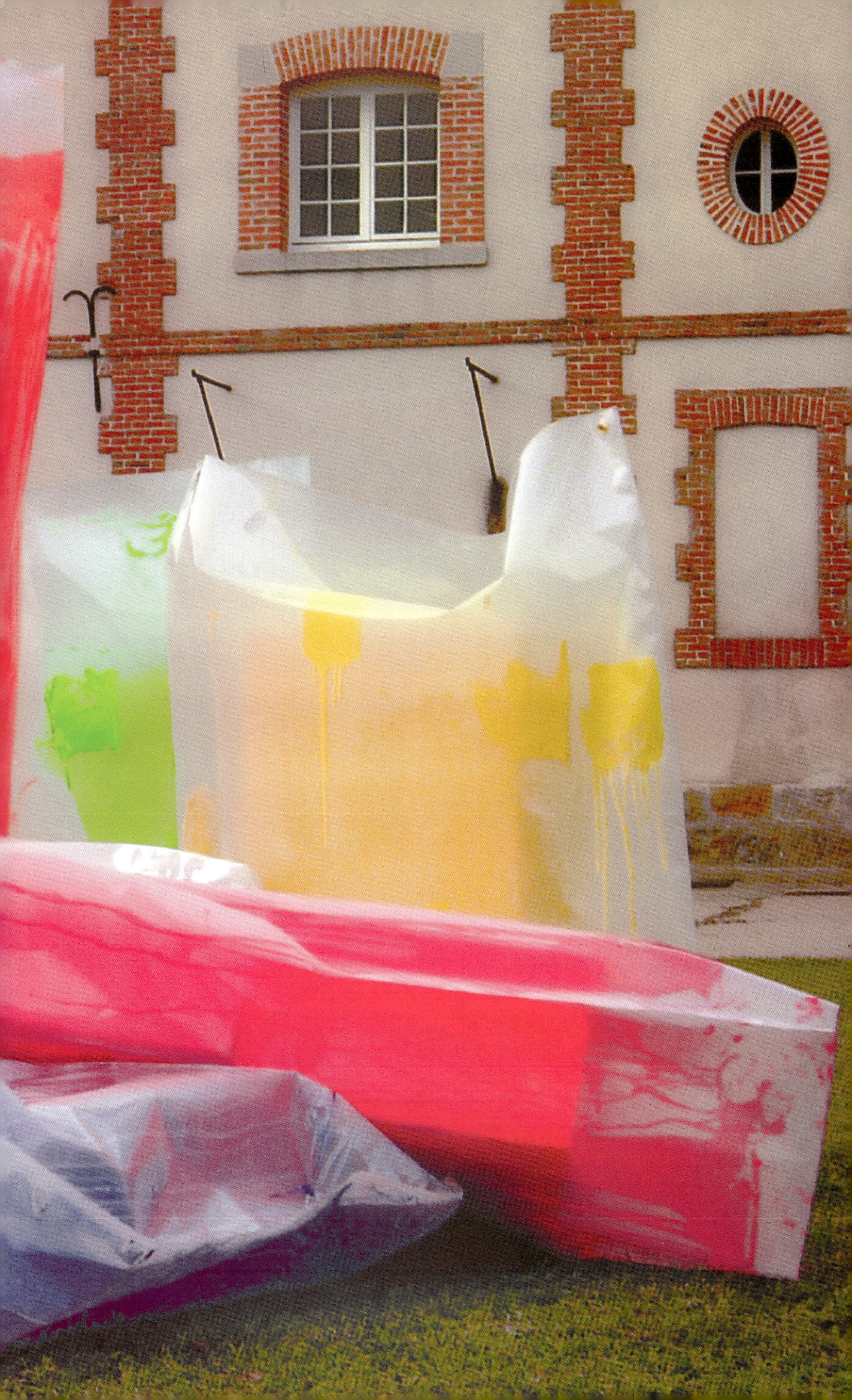

Hans

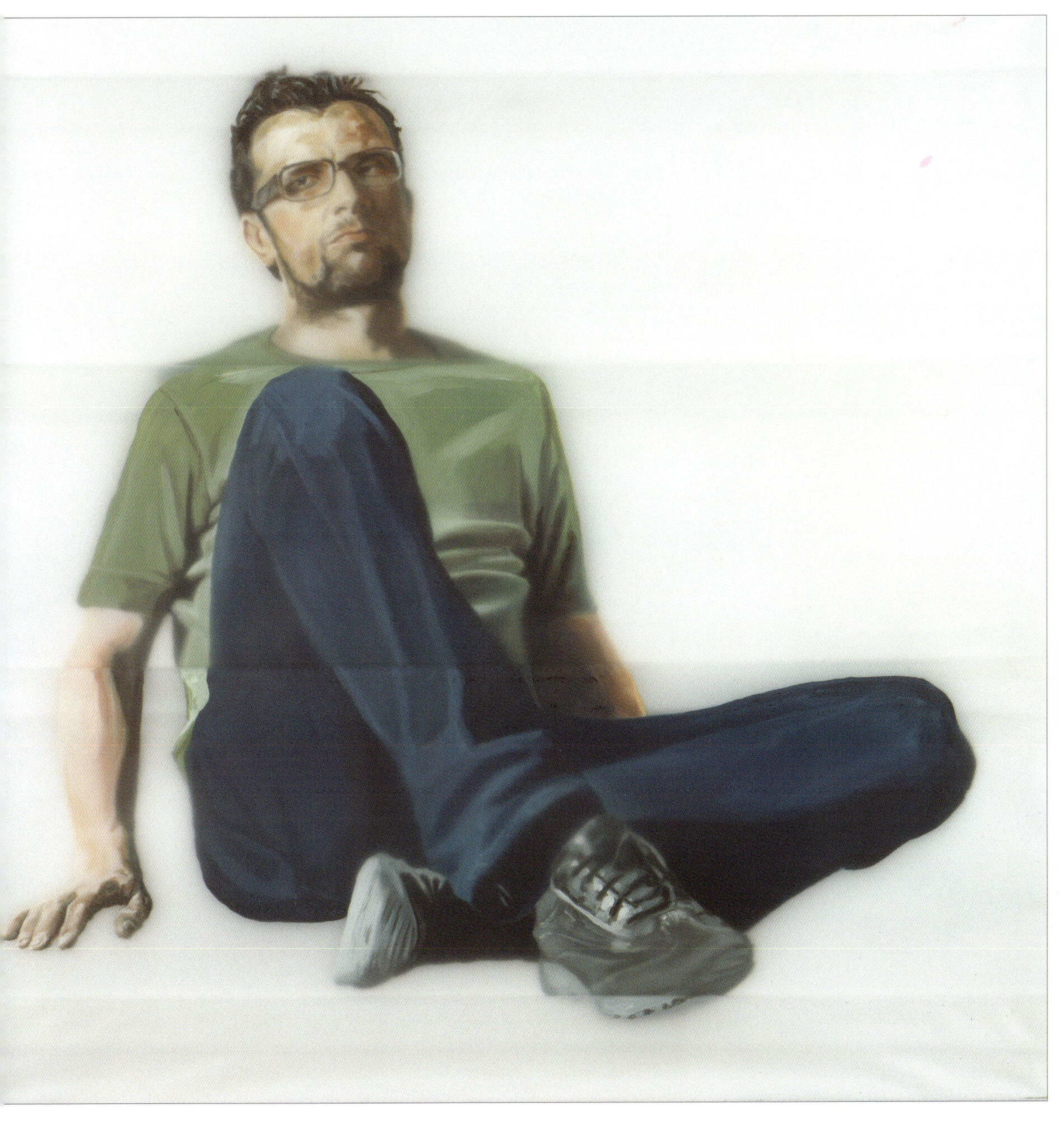

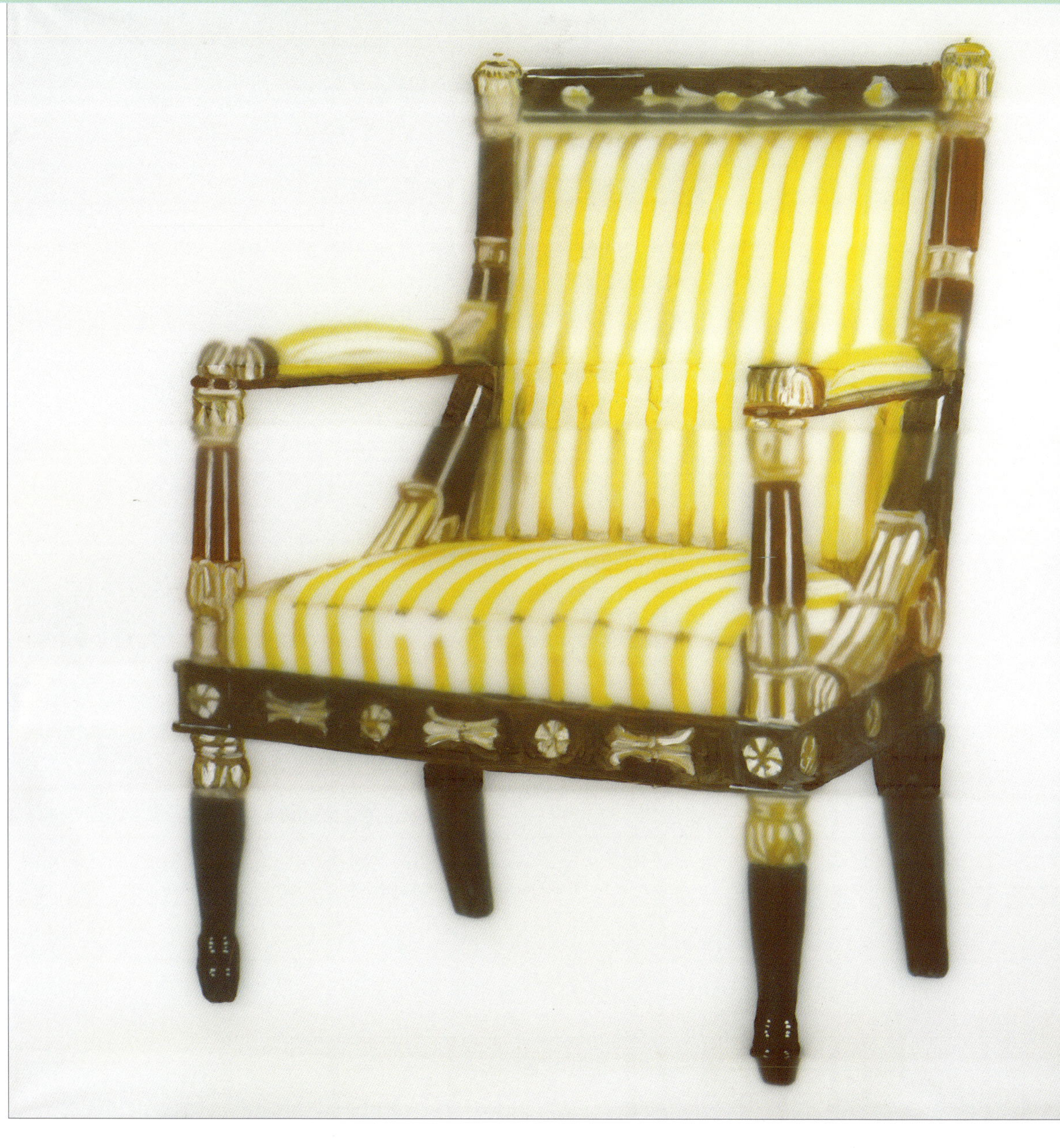

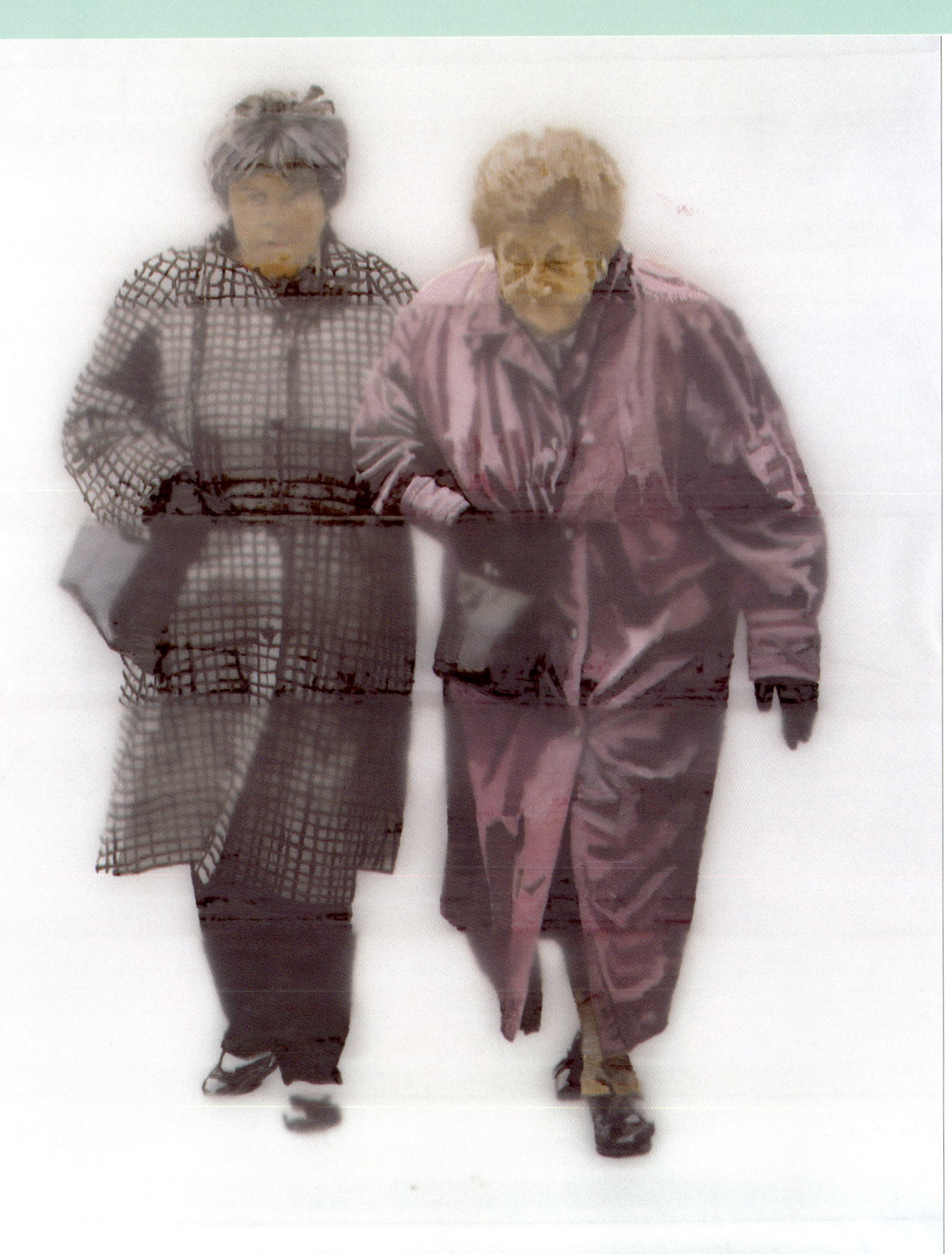

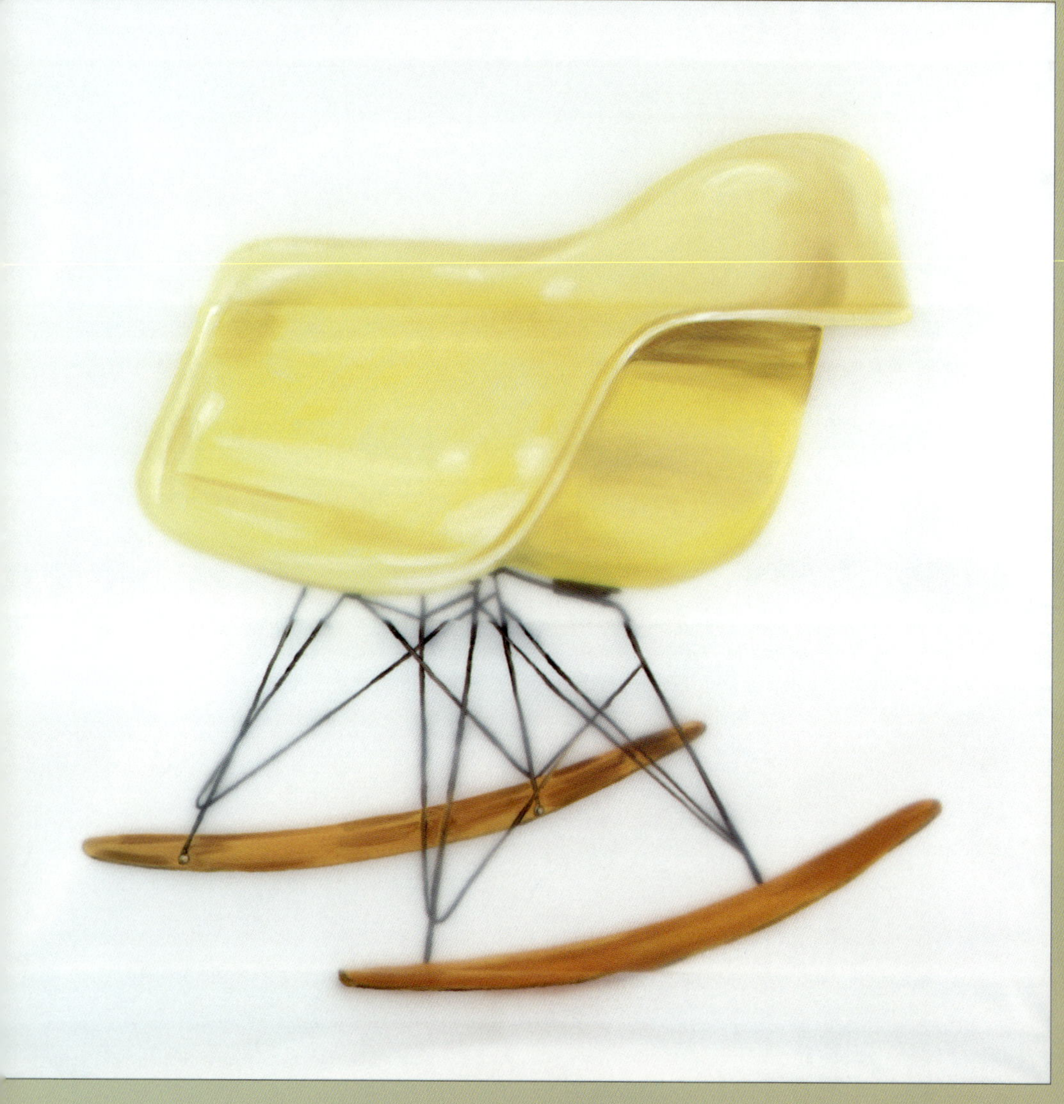

Rocking chair

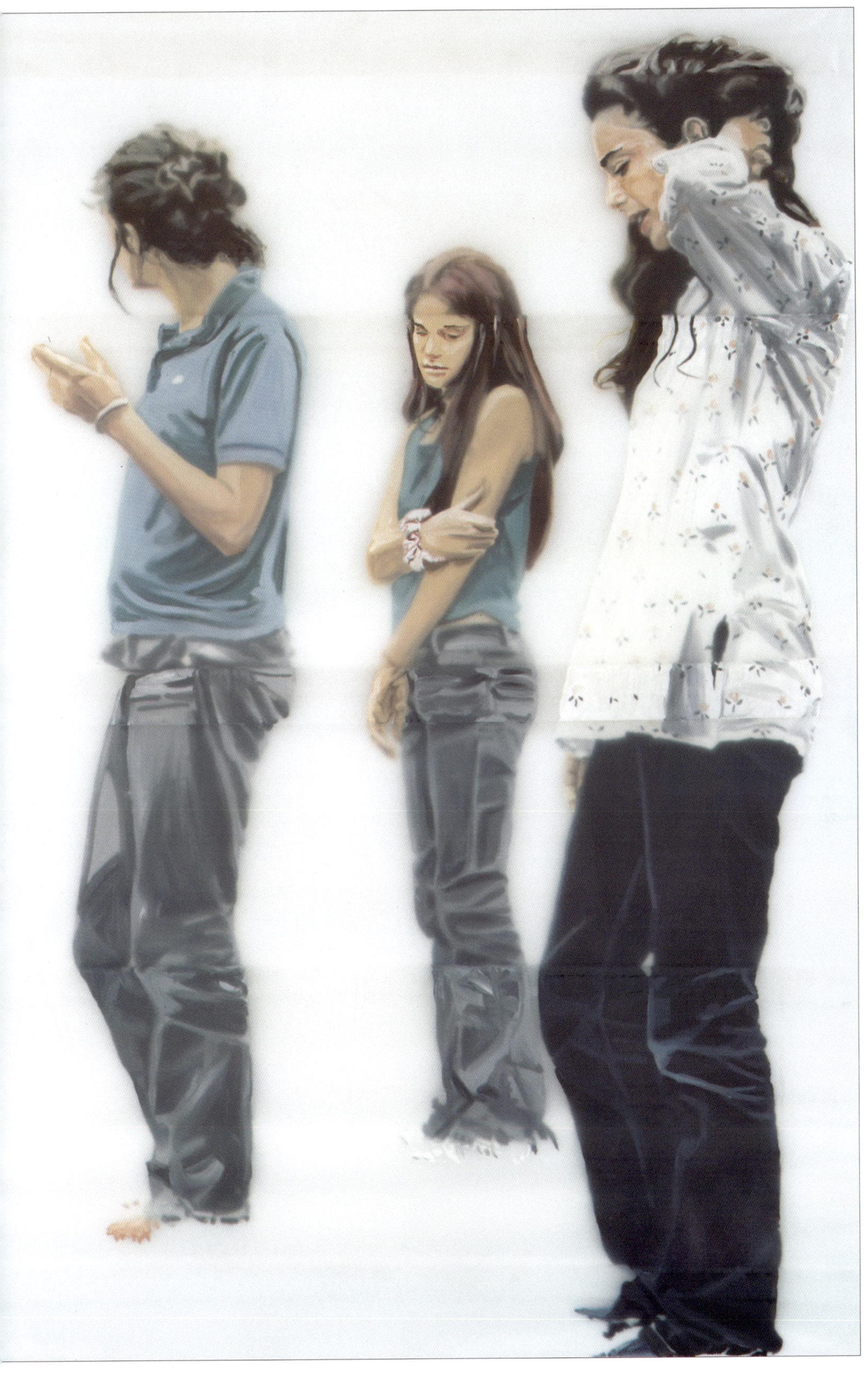

India, Laetitia and Clotilde

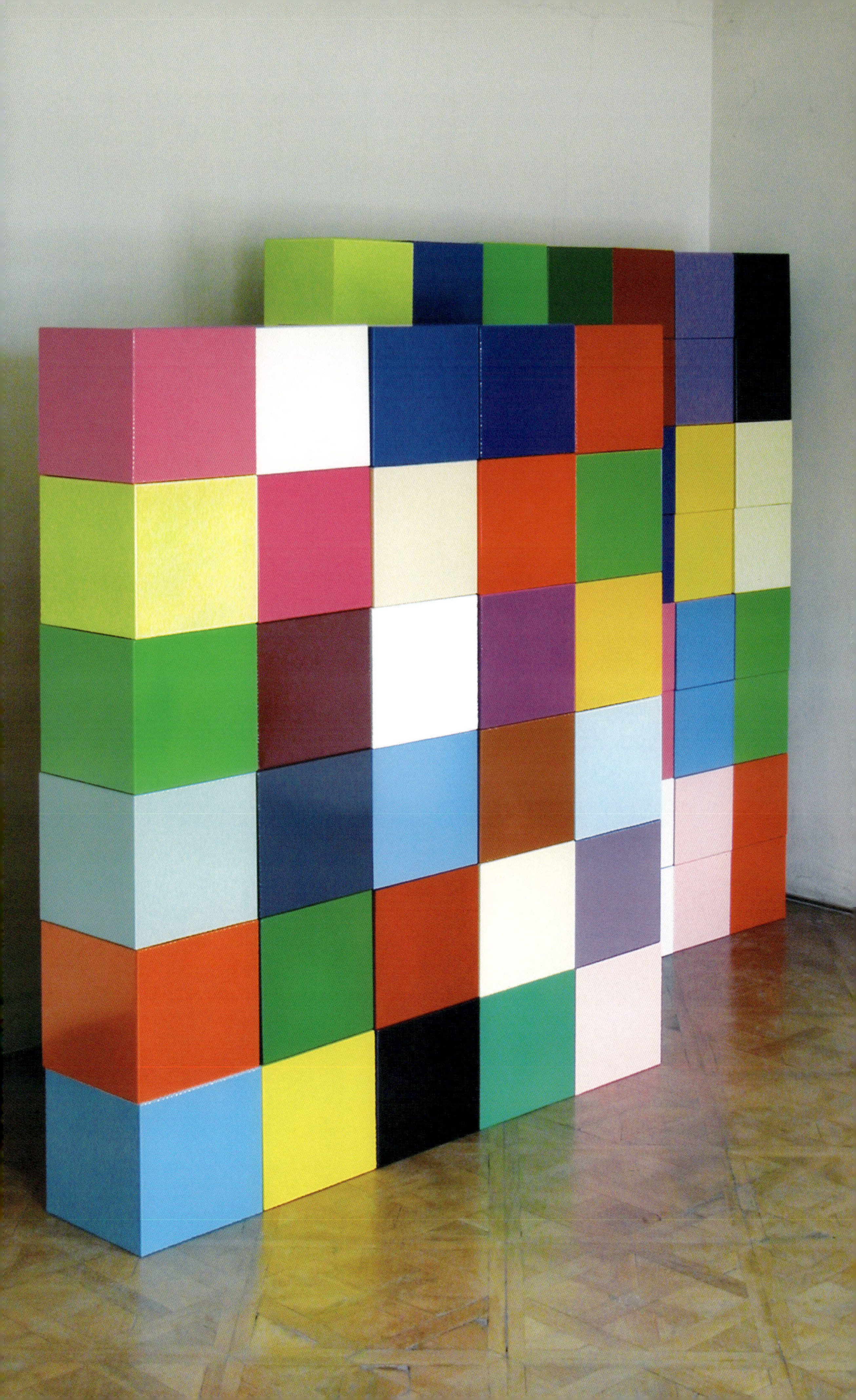

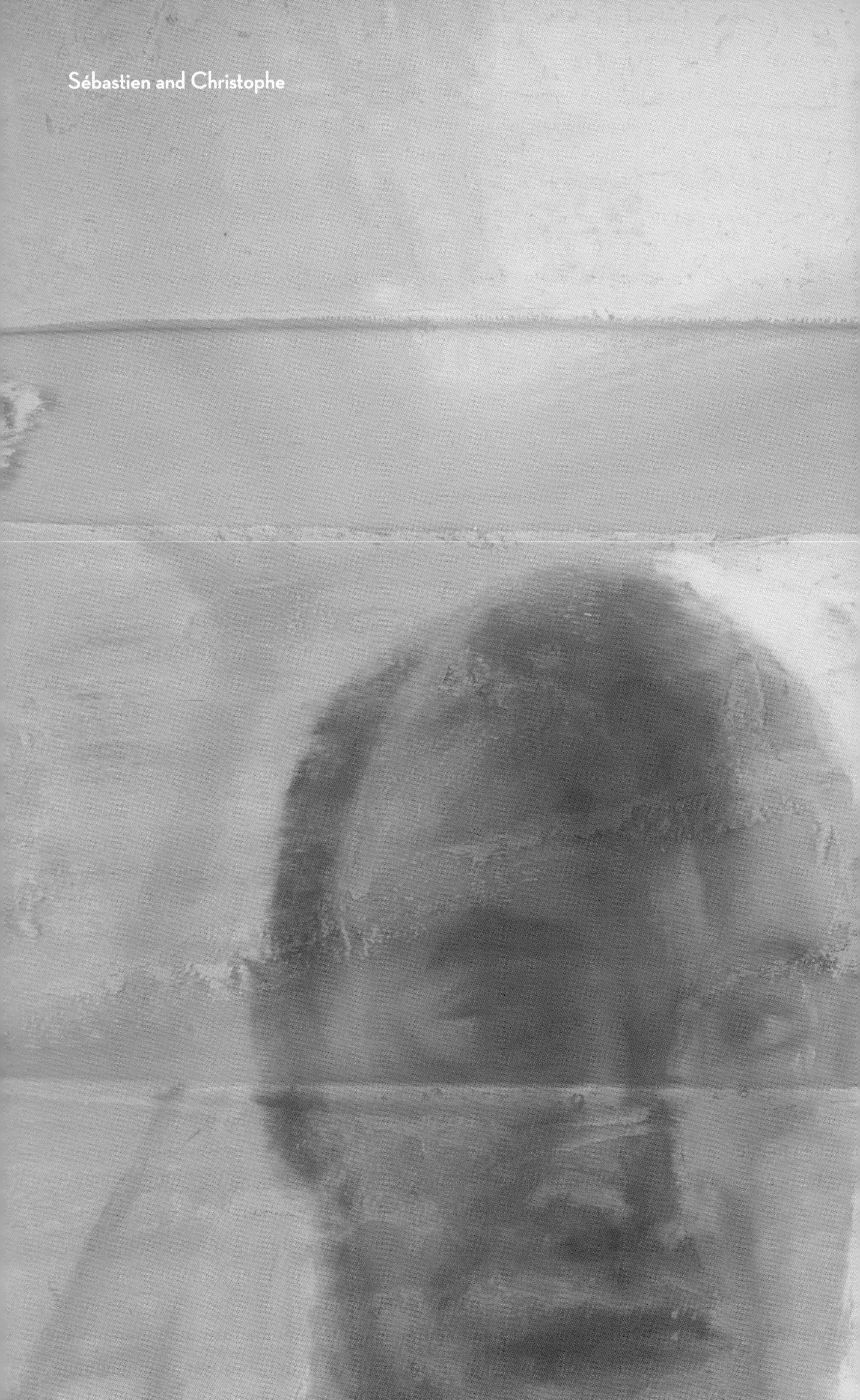
Sébastien and Christophe

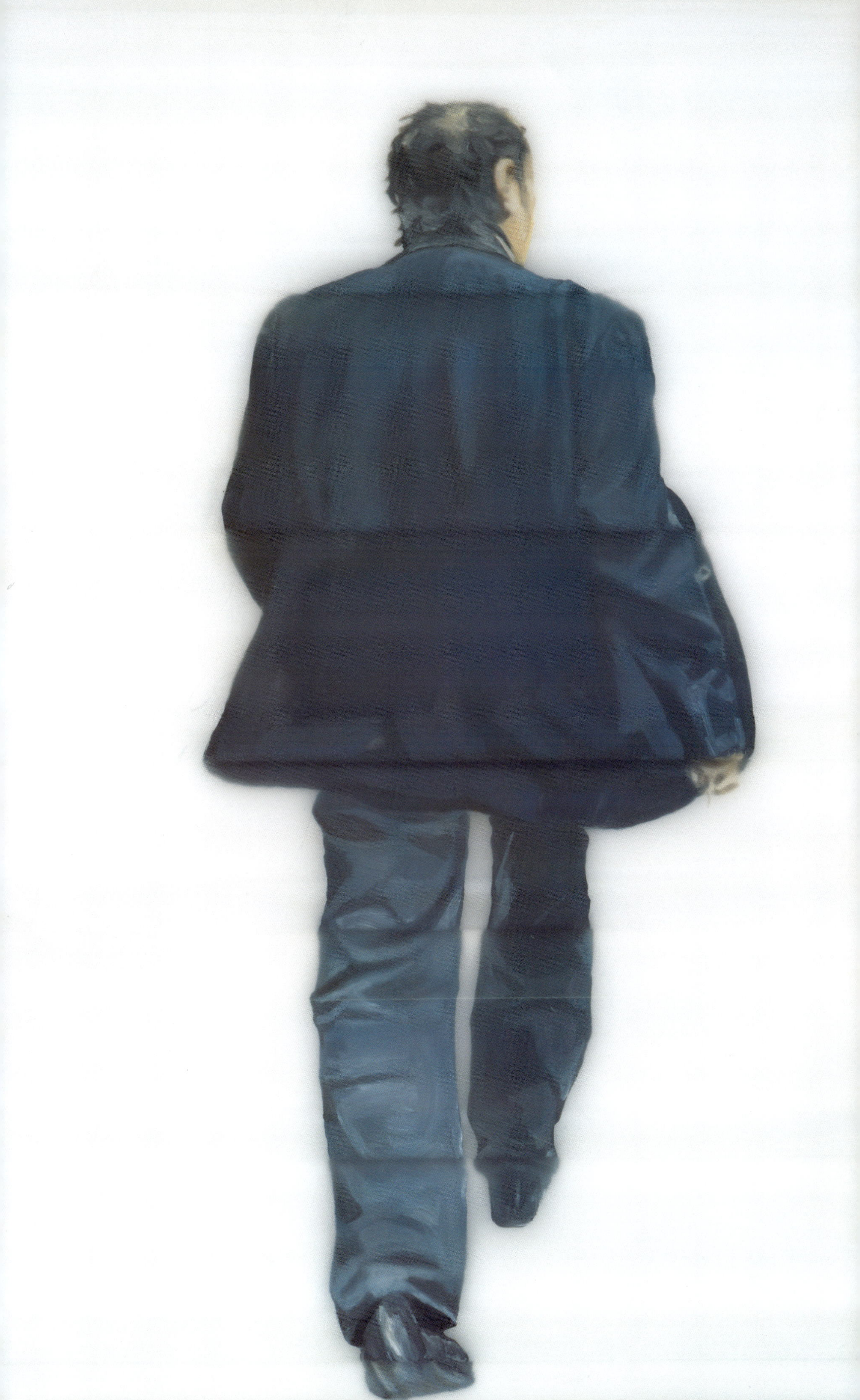

Previous pages: Katharina, Franz
Right: Gretchen

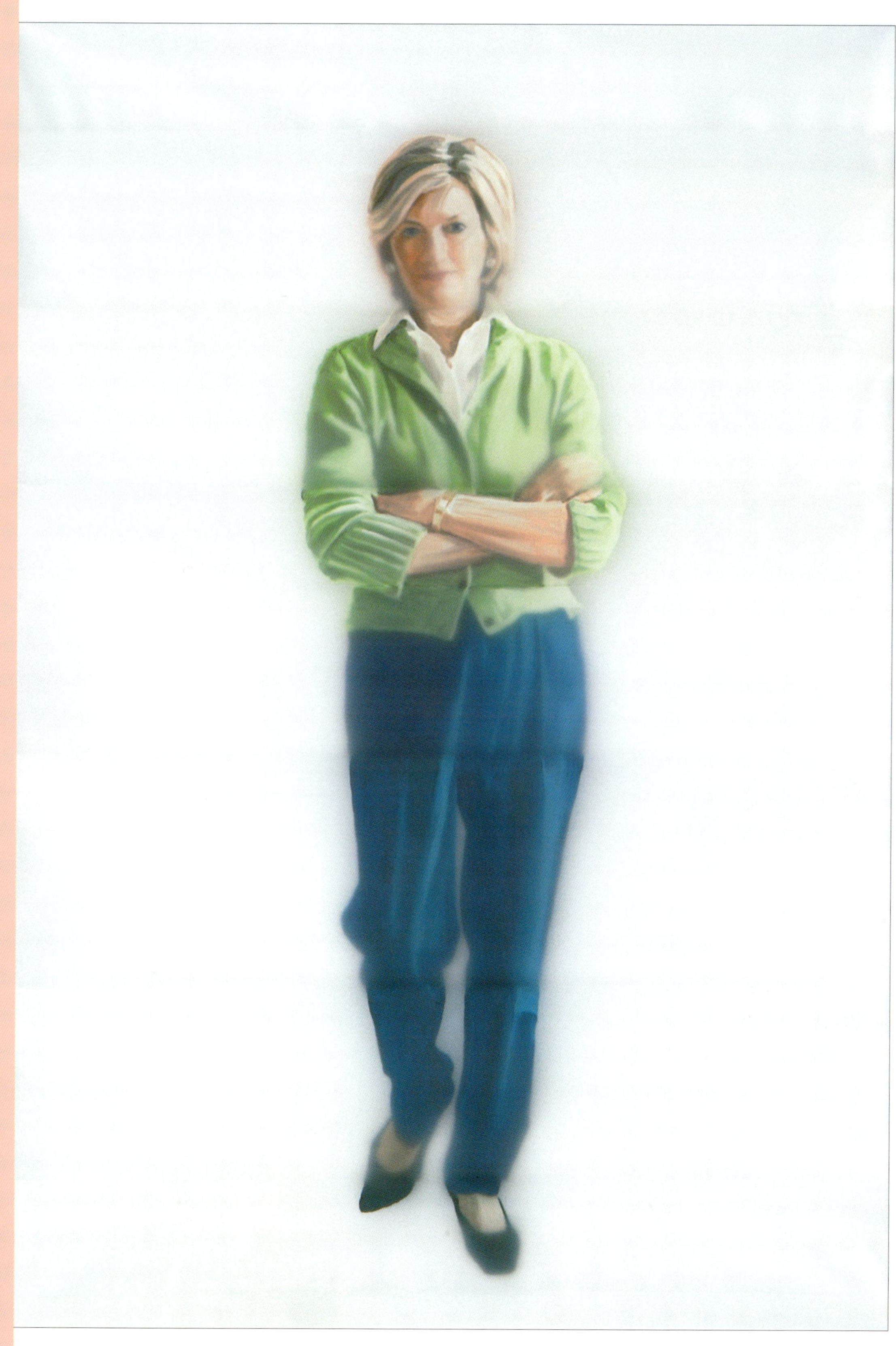

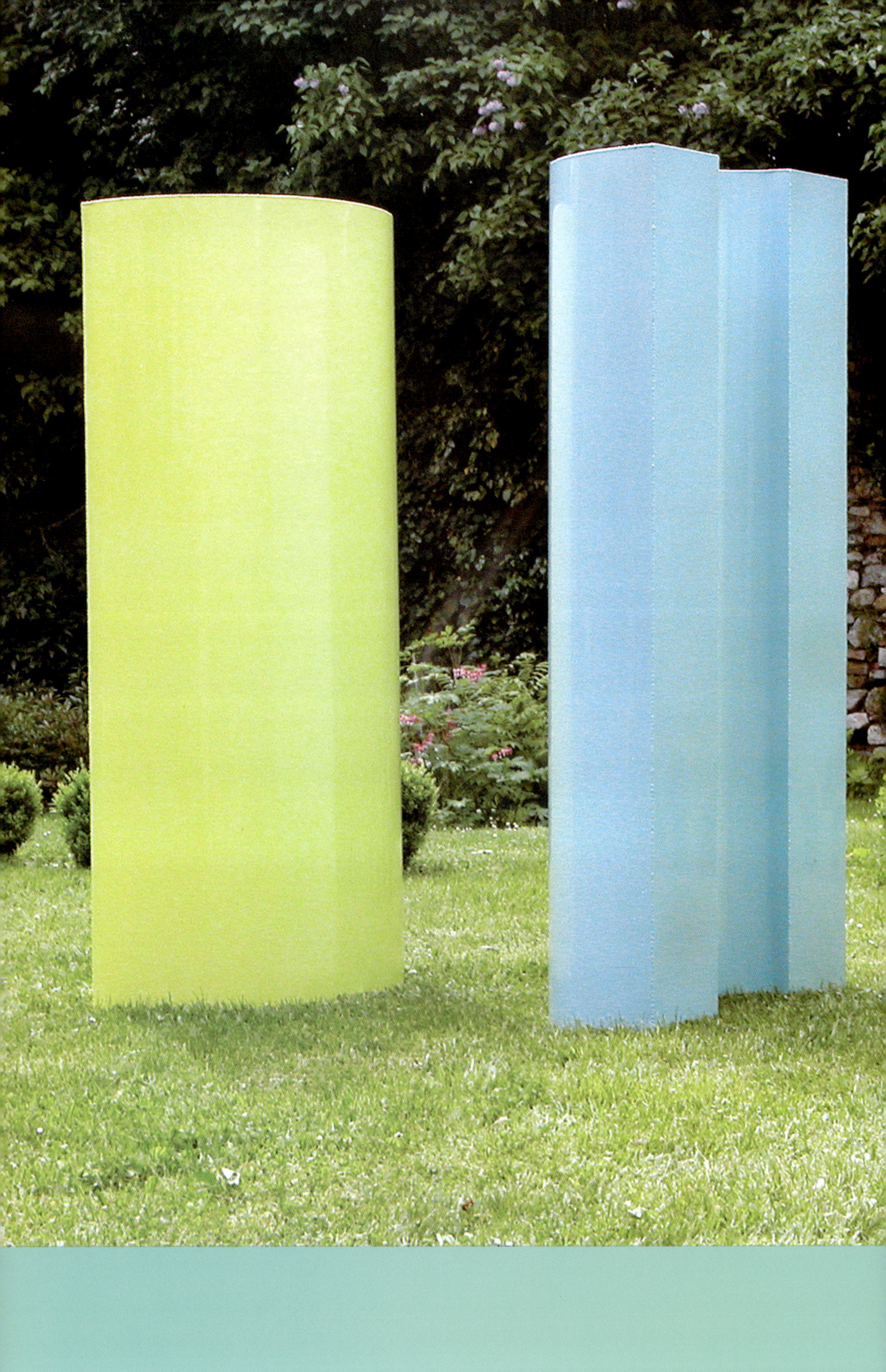

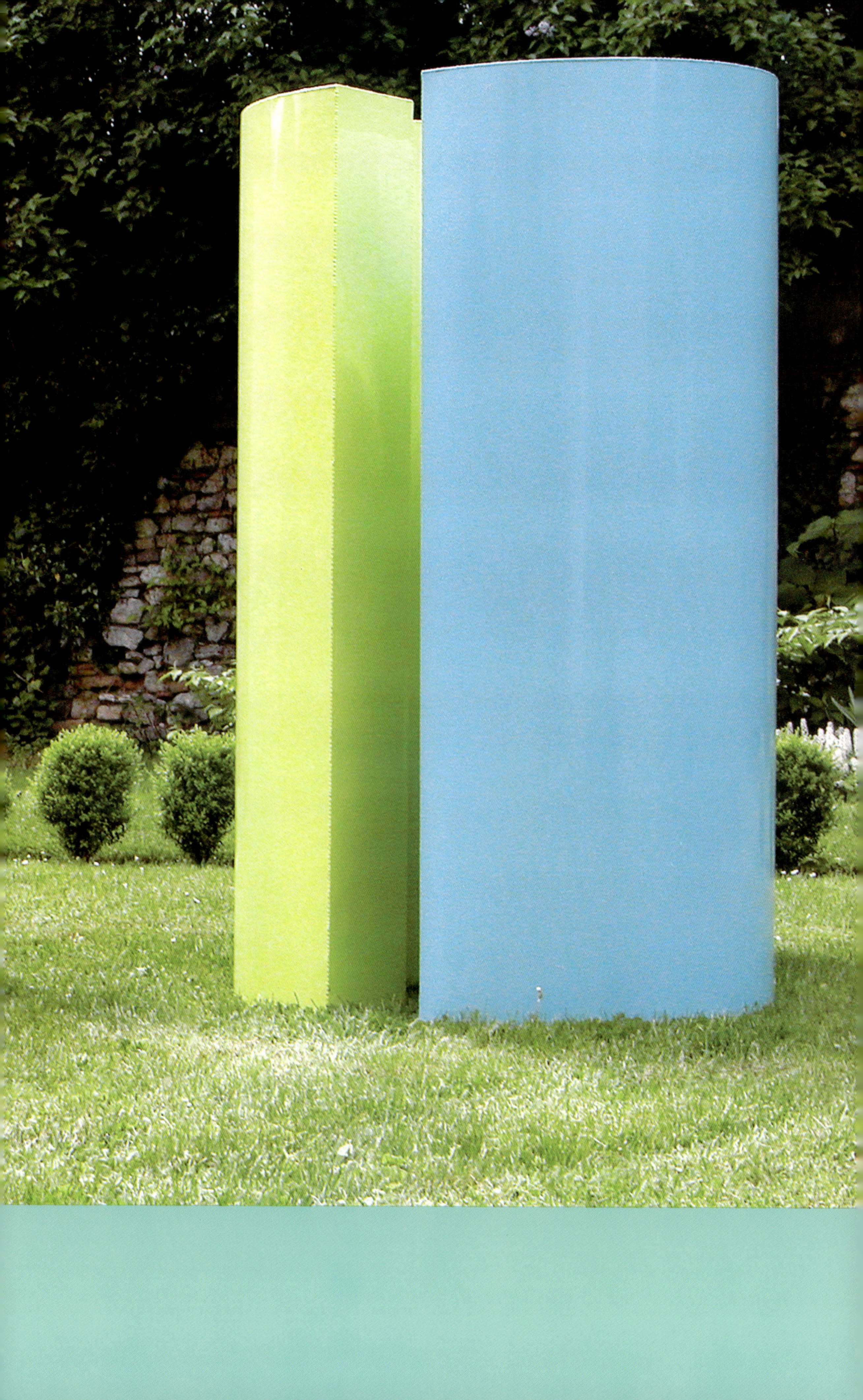

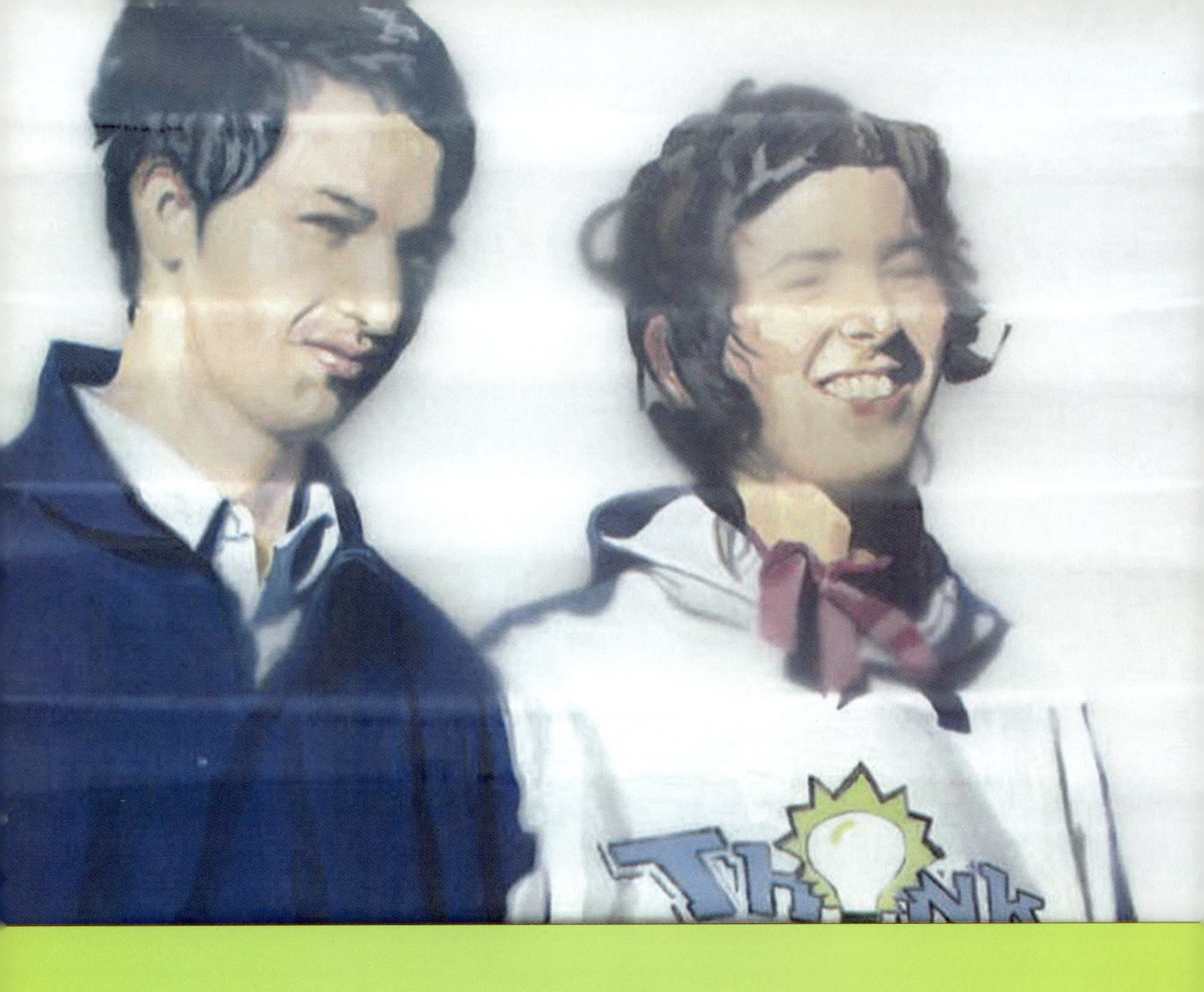
THINK

Siegrun

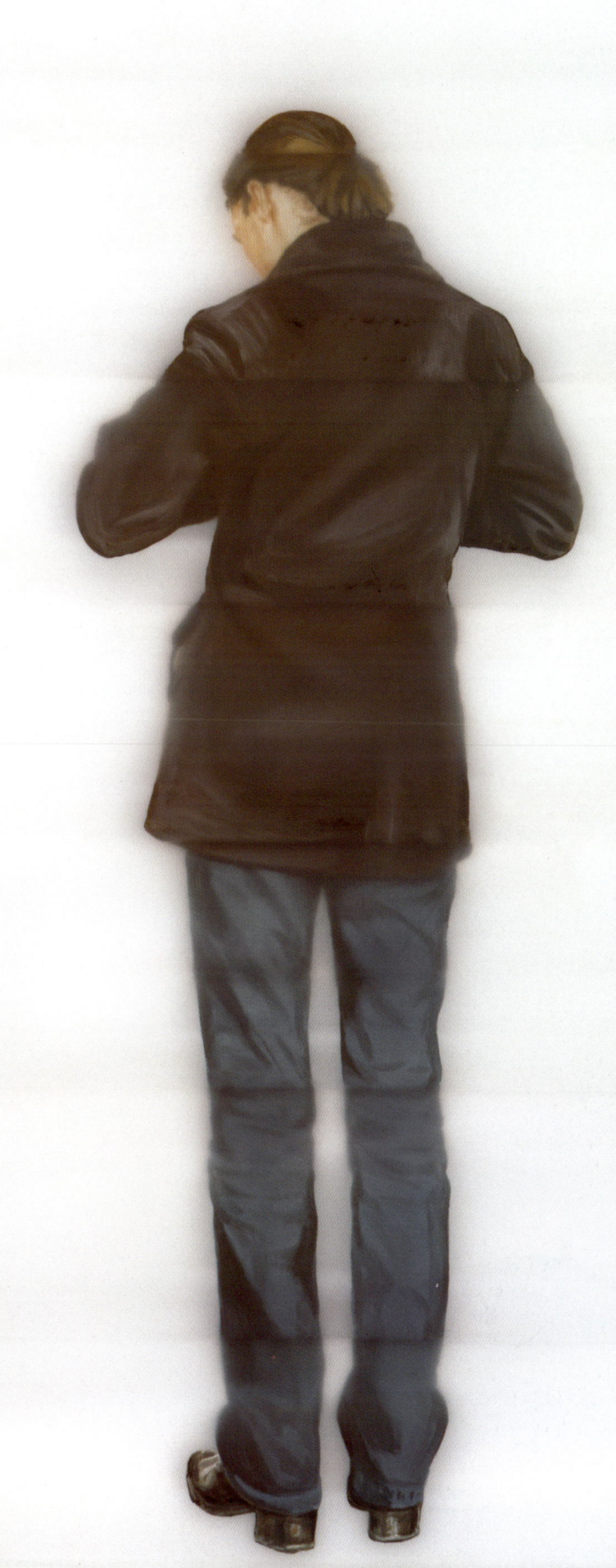

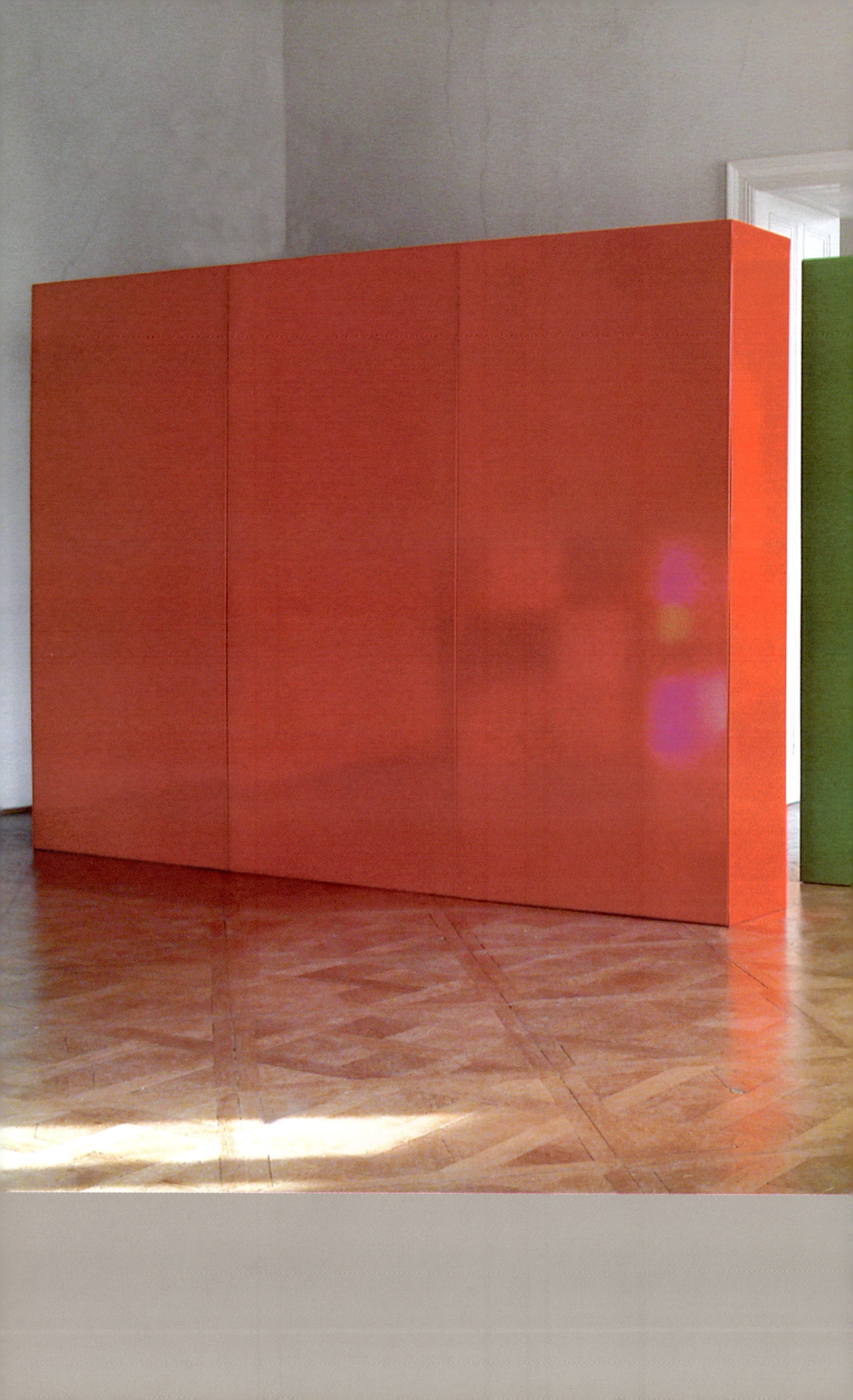

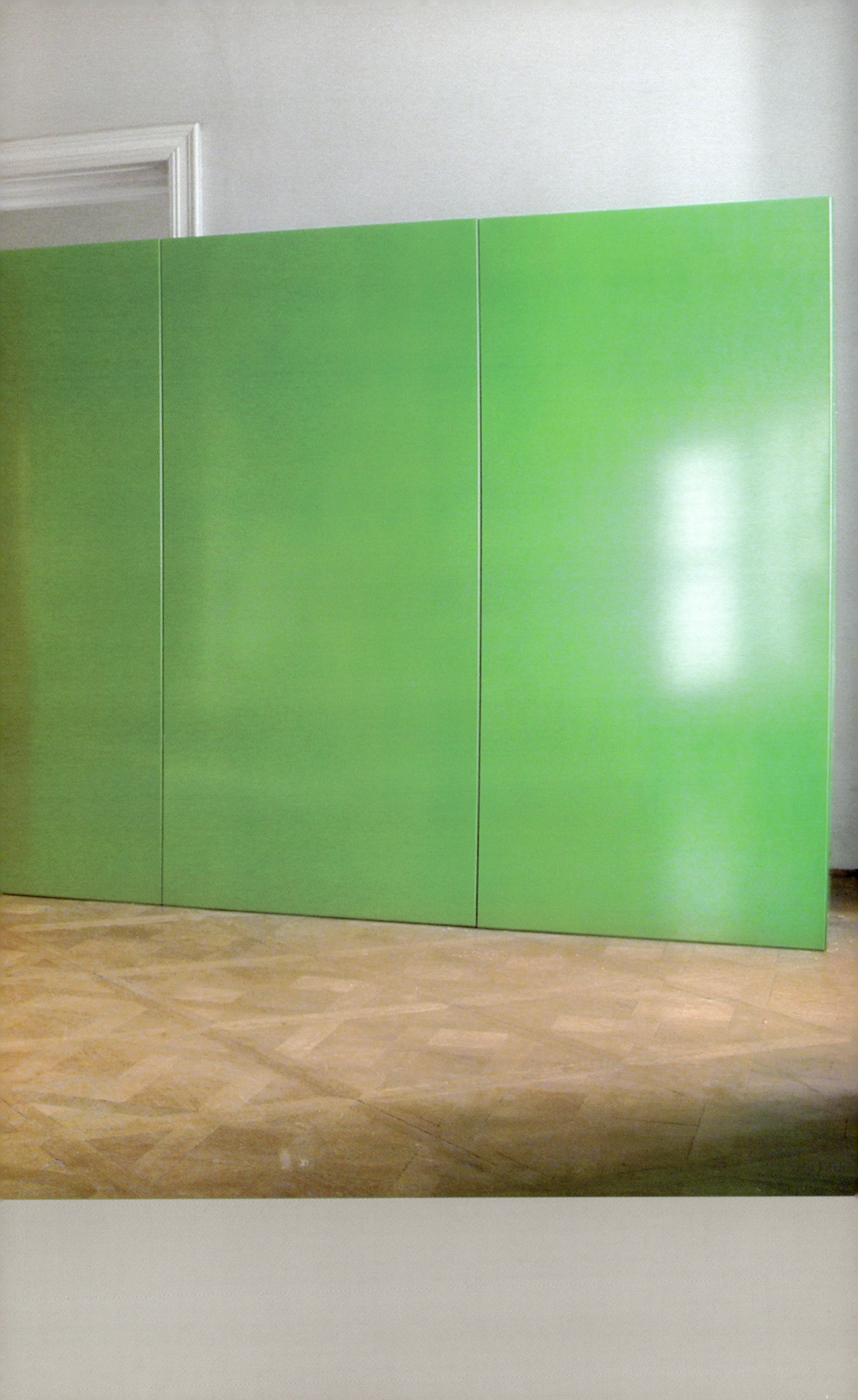

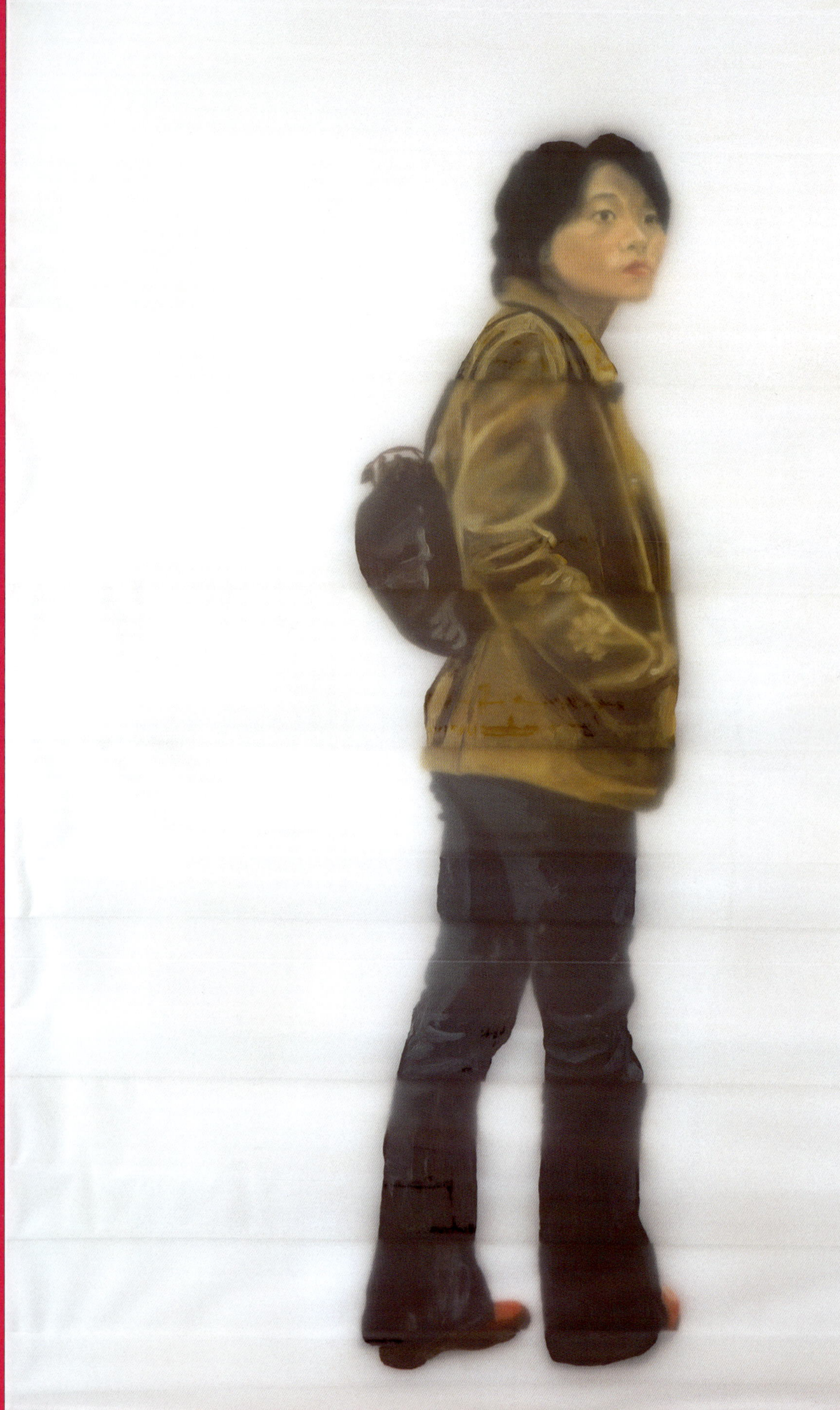

Margaux

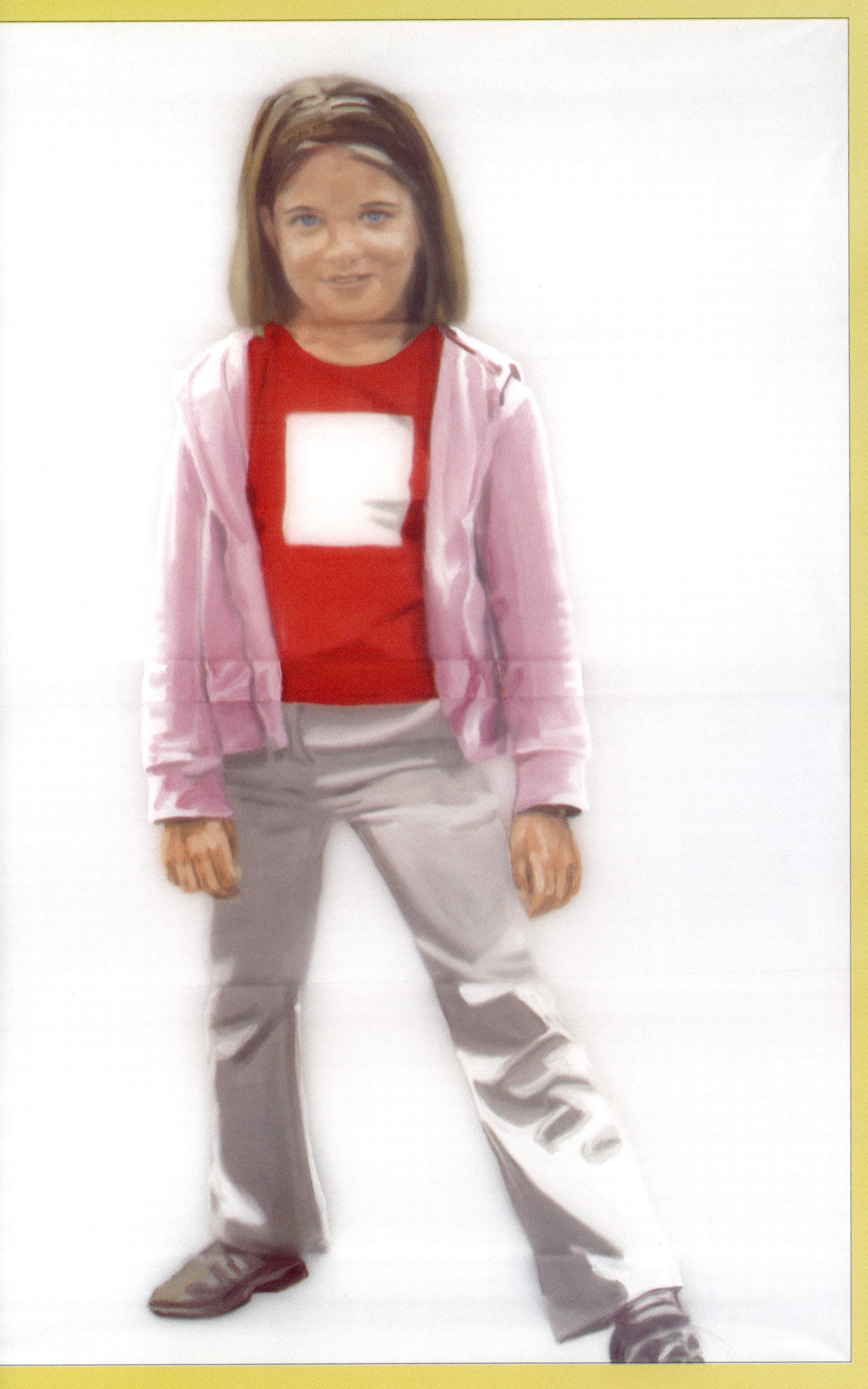

Ferdinand

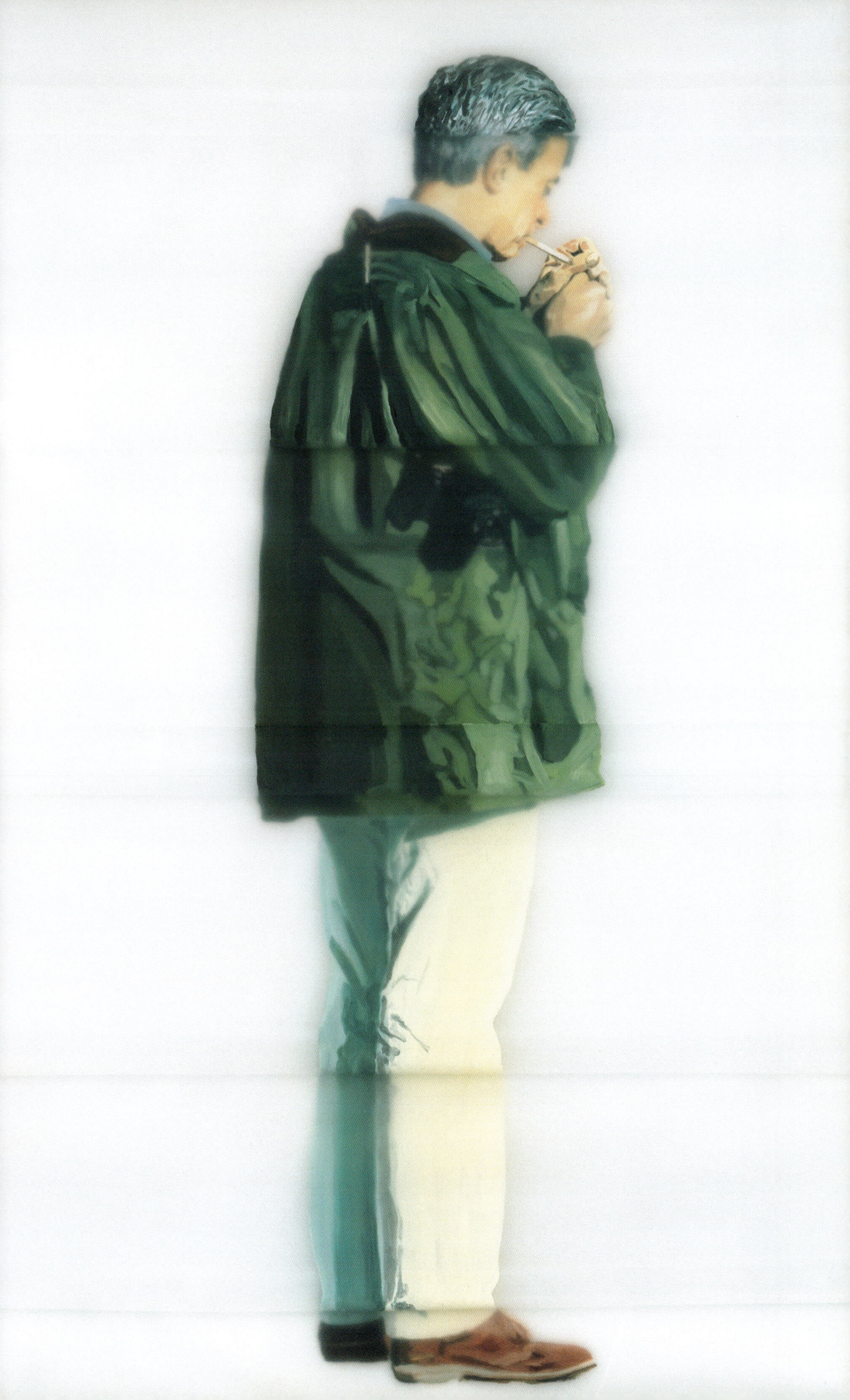

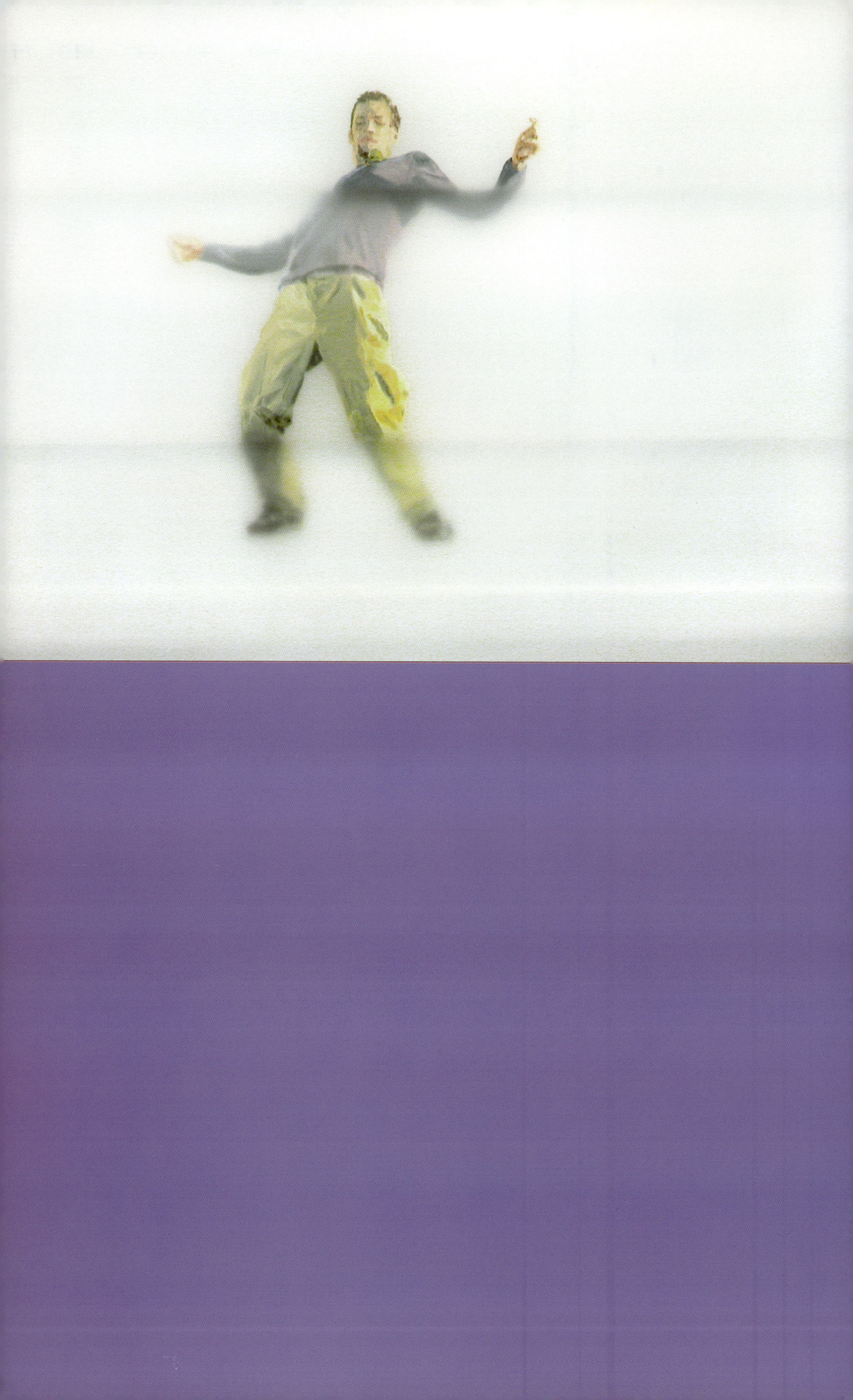

Acrobat

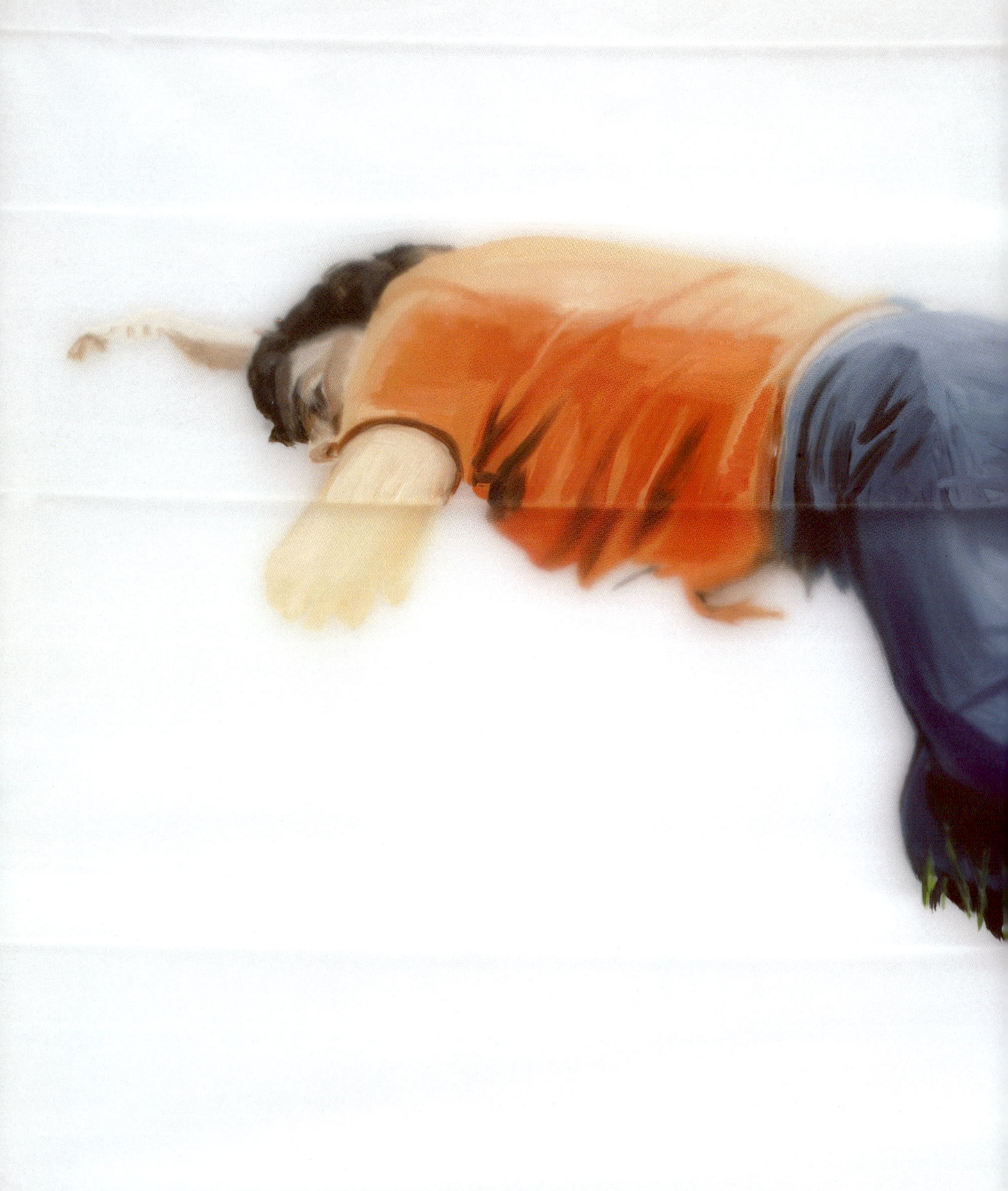

Anna

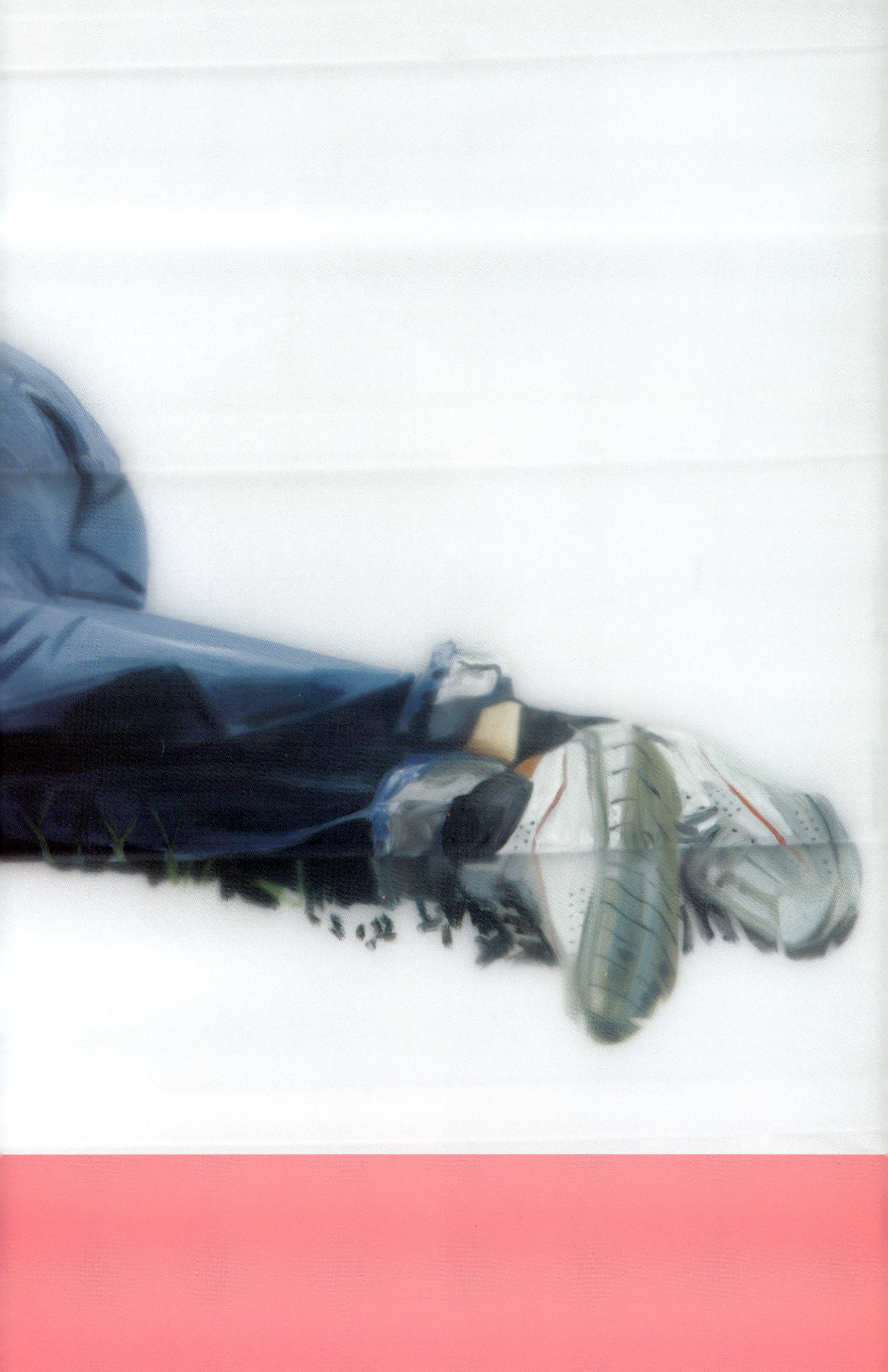

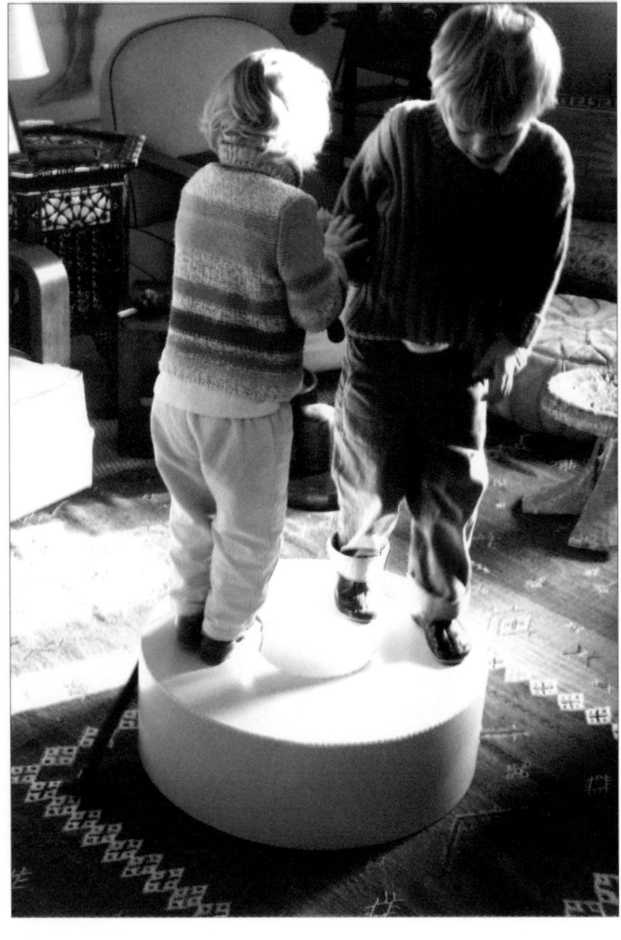

Alma and Emile dancing on *Aluminium bagel*, 2003.

Recent portraits & sculptures

An essay on Sébatien de Ganay's recent works by Richard Dailey

Sébastien de Ganay's recent work will intrigue you, if it hasn't already. For one thing, in the last couple of years he has almost single-handedly freed minimalism from its doctrinal shackles with his sculpture installations[1]. The ultra-cool logic of Judd & company's endgame in the lofts of Soho has found new purpose in a gigantic crumbling 18th Century castle in Petronell, a small town in eastern Austria on the Slovak border, where de Ganay lives with his wife and children in an apartment comfortably stanched against the weather's corrosive effects.[2] There among the vineyards, Roman ruins and windmill energy farms, minimalism is undergoing a one-man renaissance. And this is just a small part of the story.

At hand we have Sébastien de Ganay's recent painted portraits AND sculptures. Let's insist on the conjunction to start, for reasons that will be clear. You can see immediately how sculptural his paintings are, while at the same time his sculpture installations are perfectly Greenbergian in their pure paint on aluminium (the only way you could get more pure would be to do monochrome installations, including the room[3]). The walls in particular get as flat as sculpture can get from certain angles. And then in de Ganay's portraits are the trademark folds of plastic which literally create waves of relief, the balanced push-pull/ background-figure effect, the luminous white[4] void of a background over which all the figures float and by which

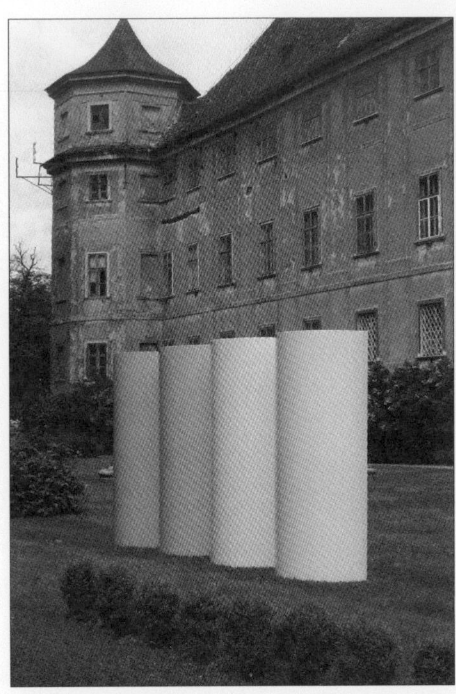

Cylinders in the park of Petronell.

they are supported, but de Ganay also layers on the paint heavily, etching his gestures in pigment. The closer you get the more the paint thickly insists on itself as heavy-duty brushstrokes.[5] Whereas in the *walls*, *cubes*, *cylinders*, and *circles* (like steel donuts) of de Ganay's sculptures with their bright car-paint monochromes we see geometric picture planes, curved or not, which foreground (particularly against the walls and cubes) the viewer almost like the figures in the paintings against their Ganay white voids, as if those figures suddenly found themselves freed from the veil of the painter's g(l)aze. Seen like this, we are all de Ganays.

Furthermore, these recent pieces are the result of more than 10 years of well-documented exploration of the relationship between painting and sculpture during which de Ganay has mined this juncture with all the means at his disposal[6]. The result is a suddenly massive resonance in his new work that startles you until you realize just how much meticulous attention, time and thought have been put into getting us here. De Ganay's new work has been brewing for a long time, but the effort is now no longer an issue: this artist whistles while he works.

Portraits first.

Before viewing de Ganay's recent work, I would have told anyone who bothered to ask that portrait painting was a double dead end, personal likeness in painting having been finished off in the early rounds by cameras, while paint itself shriveled a decade or two ago to only one option on the conceptual palette.[7] So what is it about these paintings? How is it that they make plastic and paint look so pertinent?

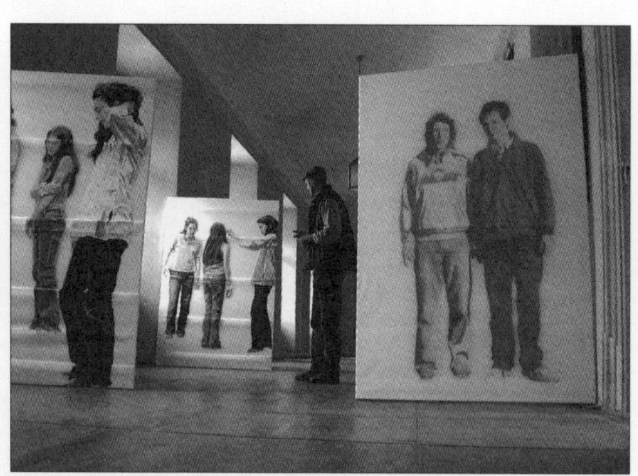

Work in progress in Petronell's corridor.

Their cool temperatures are one thing. The Ganay white backgrounds are an eye bath of light that stimulates and soothes at the same time. De Ganay is operating on many different levels in these portraits, starting with these backgrounds that shout 'studio' at first glance and then soften as they self-enrich. They contrast and support the informal poses, snapshots really, imbued with the sense that de Ganay gives us of having caught his subjects in unguarded moments. While isolating and heightening his subjects like studio portraits, these backgrounds function in exactly the opposite manner that, say, Gap advertising, or even Irving Penn's portraits of aborigines, do. That studio white was invented to create crisp cutouts, while Ganay white is as ambiguous an element as a dream. It's like deep water in that it supports the figures and yet looks capable of completely absorbing them. When the final veiling layer of plastic is layered on[8], sometimes over still wet paint (insisting further that this is paint), the effect is serenely eerie: the figures look suspended in their fields.

And then there is their silence, enhanced by the background and final plastic veil, which, crossed with the narrative insistence of their figures, also makes one think of photographs. As the artist puts it, we feel like the painted figure is inside a bubble, which confronts two worlds, our noisy one and the one of the person portrayed, silent."9 Just compare the effect here to that of Pistoletto's well-known mirror pieces, where the founder of *Arte Povera* silk-screened figures onto mirrors. Pistoletto's pieces are "noisy," meaning that the mirrors include the viewer and everything around him/her. The Ganay white background absorbs everything and liquidates any spatial reference. The notion of time/epoch is only betrayed by what the people are wearing.

In fact, de Ganay is working with a certain zeitgeist here, frankly artful portraits in the sense of Ruff and Struth, Wall and Tina Barney, or, alternatively, "found" portraits such as Streuli takes, except de Ganay is working in a totally different medium from these photographers. Yet his portraits, especially before their plastic veils are applied, are almost photorealist from the right distance, an astonishing feat considering the economy of gesture in de Ganay's paintings. De Ganay works fast, rendering them in an unbelievable 3 hours on average. Of course he goes back after the heat of the moment and retouches them where necessary, but still the astonishing ratio of intense economy of gesture to power of visual impact hits right where we like it. And isn't there is something of the charming simplicity of Alex Katz's work here, too ? Finally all of the allusions resolve themselves behind that quiet veil.

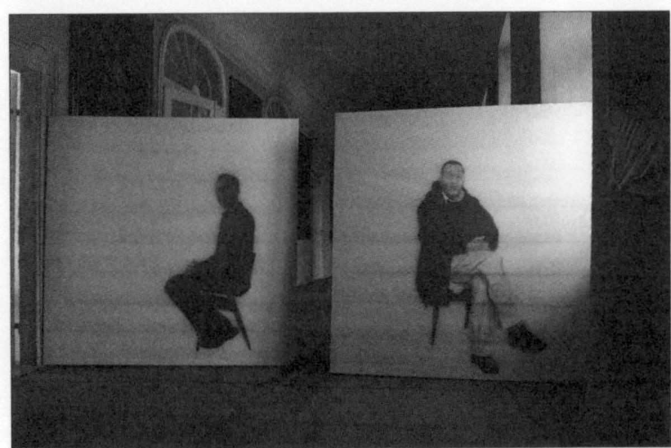

Left: **Erwin**, right: **Christophe**, 2003

Sheer visual and narrative intrigue are also part of our pleasure in these paintings. Visually, they fill the eye but refuse to lie still, playing with our normal efforts to locate the picture plane. They undulate, or they shift forward and back. Newcomers to de Ganay's technique may even find themselves blinking as they begin to dissect the initial visual impression. The more you look, the more you wonder how it was done.10 And out of that visual game, narrative and contextual questions are in turn provoked by the subjects and then frustrated by the denuded circumstances until the mind, tantalized, can't help but try to fill the void. Who are these people? Where are they? What is that guy thinking about as he sits in his chair ("seated man in blue jacket")? Who is the smiling man waving at ("man looking out through a window")? What's with the old women, so familiar and so unsettling at the same time ("old women walking")? The viewer's pleasure is further enhanced when he/she realizes the game has been deliberately constructed to remain open ended, that our imaginations have been subtly and willingly engaged in a kind of perpetual play. De Ganay's sense of play is profound, and I'll get back to it when discussing his sculpture.

Which brings us to the subjects of these paintings: people and chairs. Here's another built-in contradiction: the intimacy we feel with de Ganay's subjects in spite of (or because of) their extreme isolation. The effect is diametrically opposed to that of the aristocratic oil paintings in the portrait gallery next to which he works, and perhaps this in itself is de Ganay's answer to tradition. What we do know are de Ganay's subjects, or feel we might, even if we never will. In fact, you may recognize one or even many of these people, but ultimately it doesn't matter. They are palpably human. They wear Gap as well as Yves Saint Laurent. They smoke. They take pictures. They throw

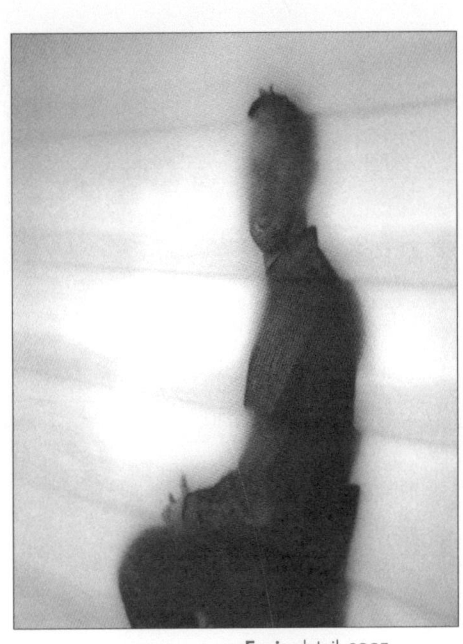

Erwin, detail, 2003

sand at the beach. They touch. They wave goodbye. They suffer and they love. De Ganay has produced a revealing slice of life for us. Even his chairs feel imbued with personality; and let's not overlook the marvelous bilingual word play in the word "chair," which means flesh in French. De Ganay's sense of play isn't limited to the visual.

And then the size of these paintings, particularly the big ones, feels right, especially when they are hung away from the wall or on hinges, which sets them at a variable angle to it. Their size forces us to take them seriously without imposing unpleasantness; it also tells us that these paintings have been made to be lived with and not simply stashed away in museums. And de Ganay's conceptual engine is running in tune here too: real size becomes a questionable concept under the circumstances, particularly when our artist begins scaling small figures (children) large and vice versa, as he has very recently begun doing.[11]

Most people will assume, rightly, that these portraits are of De Ganay's friends and family, just as we get that immediately about Nan Goldin's portraits of her world or Tina Barney's of hers. And de Ganay, like Barney and all those other photographers, gives us his world as he finds it.[12] The more you look at these portraits, the more radical that becomes.

Now Sculptures.

Impeccable pedigree is the first thing about de Ganay's recent sculptures that will strike anyone who remembers Conceptual art's analytical offspring, Minimalism. De Ganay spent his art school years in New York City in the 1980s, a decade that saw the apotheosis of Donald Judd. And De Ganay has in part spent the last 4 years trying to liberate sculpture[13] (without sawing any cows in half) from the deep systematic hole Minimalism had dug for it, and now he has circled back to meet it again on his own terms. His approach is similar but critically different from the generation of artists like John McCraken (with his "surfboards"), who grew out of minimalism in the 60s.[14] In de Ganay's painted aluminium *walls*, *cubes*, *donuts*, and sliced *cylinders* are all the pure anonymity the bad-ass monks of Minimalism could possibly require. And yet something is different. This work just doesn't feel like another branch on the same old logic tree, it feels like one of those conceptual hybrids that open visual vistas: industrial leggo? And what has happened to Minimalism's glinting severity, its unyielding rigor, its humorless analytical reductionism? How has de Ganay managed to humanize the sight of aluminium and paint?

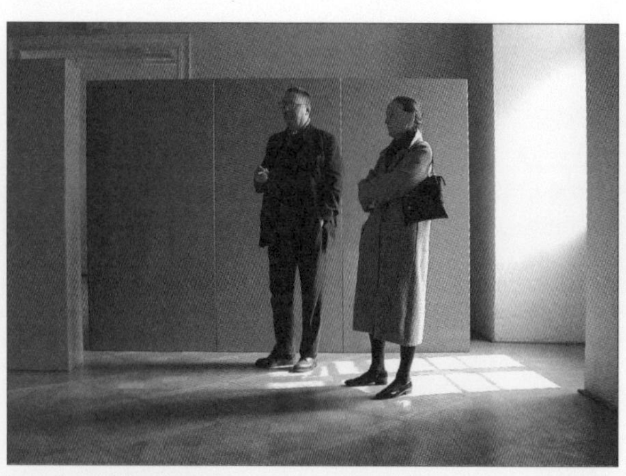
Rudolf and Siegrun in front of **Walls**, 2003.

Leaving aside for a moment the eye-pleasing power of these pieces, critically speaking it is important to understand the body of de Ganay's recent sculpture as a whole. Taken together this work implies infinite variability, a promise Minimalism had forgotten, where objects over time theoretically work together to become a kind of chaos machine that will never make the same motion twice. These sculptures are all freestanding "installations" that by their nature are

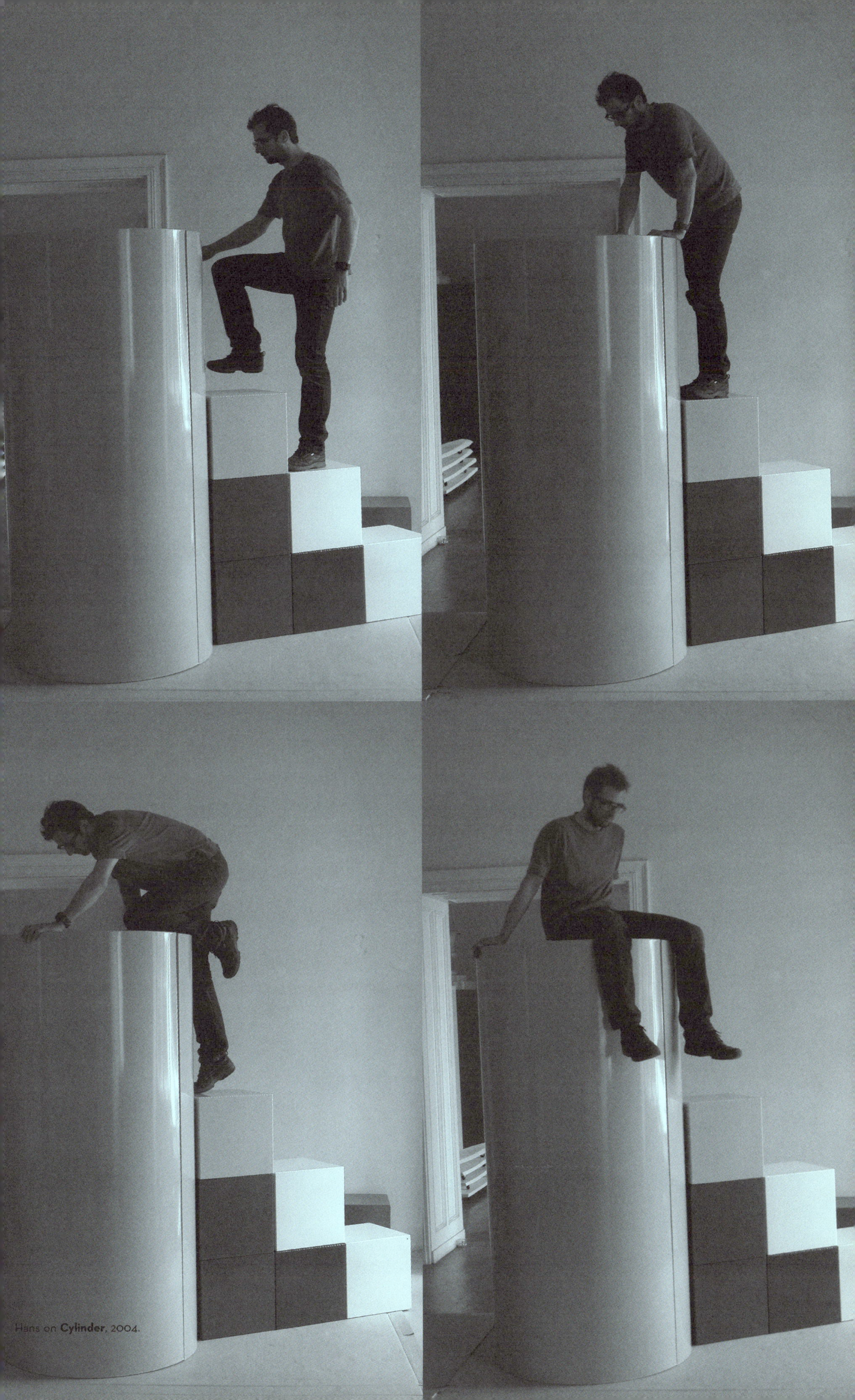

Hans on **Cylinder**, 2004.

infinitely and pleasurably variable. They are modular. Here is another critical departure from artists like McCracken. De Ganay is divisible. Mobile. Scalable. These are his conceptual tools. To see de Ganay demonstrating this principal on his concrete prototypes will do the work of many words here...

De Ganay also encourages people to bring his sculptures into their living spaces as tables or seats, and he scales his work to fit the function. Then again, his big wall pieces actually make architecture the point, and of course function is a fundamental consideration in their installation simply by virtue of their size and shape. Here de Ganay scales his work up to jumbo, public installation and museum sizes, with all his nonchalant elegance intact thanks to his old friend Minimalism.

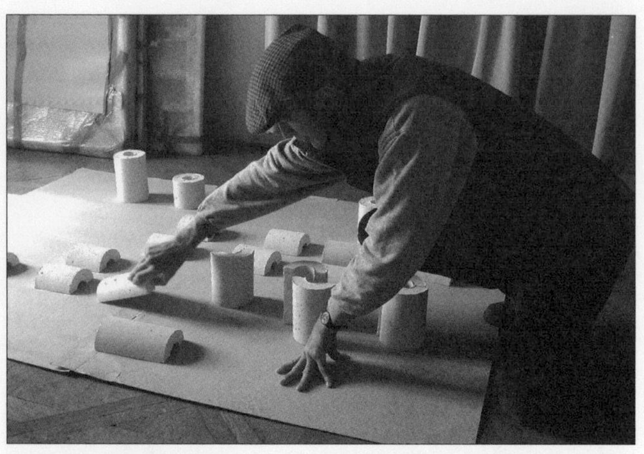
At work in the studio

There's a lot more, of course, to expound on in the way of theory here. De Ganay's roots are in the 80s, when Conceptual art (essentially art in language and language in art) went into supernova mode, and he is true to those roots even as he tends to his business on the border of Eastern Europe and in the Argentine heartland. He's playing a mind game with your eyes. Even an old color field theorist can have a good time with this stuff. Finally, though, all the critical industry on planet art couldn't help him if the material at hand wasn't so evidently eye candy of the inspired sort. Just think about walking around those monochrome, rectangular walls with their glossy, reflective surfaces: the concealing and revealing, the mysterious (in places almost crushing) intimacy amidst the gigantic planes, all the permutations of basic geometry and the way they comment on the surroundings.[15]

As with the portraits, in de Ganay's sculpture his sensibility and intelligence interact with tradition using contemporary materials and original techniques. And as I tried to point out at the start, it is at the conjuncture of sculpture and painting that Sébastien de Ganay's work really starts to resonate. Yet one is left wondering, finally, where de Ganay's sensibility will lead him next. We have not touched here on his political works, or his wide-ranging support of the arts in general. Behind his delightful sense of play lies an inquisitive mind in perpetual search of formal incarnations of artistic truths, be these the humanized verities of Minimalism or the universal particularity of his portraits.

[1] While this is demonstrably true, no artist works in a cultural vacuum. The California artist John McCraken also works in a similar vein, as will be discussed below. McCraken is onto some of the same territory as de Ganay, but the two artists are very different.

[2] The schloss actually belongs to de Ganay's wife's family, and it's state of decay is due to a long-stalled renovation.

[3] These sculptures are mostly meant to be interior installations, but they certainly work outdoors too. The biggest change in the outdoor pieces is the effect of light, which is perhaps more intense in the interior installations.

[4] Hereafter referred to as "Ganay white."

[5] De Ganay uses paint brushes, though, so please don't get the idea that he is plastering the paint on with a trowel. One of the effects he achieves this way is to widen the visual zone where paint becomes people and vise versa, an effect (not unlike slow motion in film) which further calls attention to the medium.

[6] From de Ganay's 1994 catalogue at Richard Salmon LTD in London and Galerie Jacqueline Moussion in Paris: "For he has opened up an area for work for which he is still only just beginning to impress with features, only just beginning to fold into relief." (Thierry Davila).

[7] Of course there is and always will be a commercial market for painted portraits, but that market doesn't concern us here. See for example the web site of the Royal British Academy of portrait painters.

[8] Hereafter referred to as the "veil."

[9] Sébastien de Ganay (note, 29/04/04).

[10] "The plastic paintings consist of getting a custom made plastic (one ton minimum) delivered in a roll which I stretch and pleat over canvas. After the folding is ready I paint on it. Then I cover/seal the whole with a last layer of plastic which I paint over with an anti UV varnish made for pvc/plastics." Sébastien de Ganay, email 6/04/04.

[11] I can't resist relating that when I visited de Ganay in Petronell in preparation for this article, we leaned all of his paintings against the walls in his in-law's portrait gallery, a windowed corridor perhaps 70 meters long, 6 meters wide, and five meters high, presided over by a dozen or so august 17th and 18th century types and a few historical scenes. The effect was a knockout, in part because it became obvious how successfully de Ganay has updated one of painting oldest and most venerated genres.

[12] The world of each of these artists is radically different, obviously, as different as photography and painting. De Ganay is no voyeur, finally; he disembeds his subjects from their social context in search of a degree of abstraction that perhaps invites a deeper recognition of oneself in the other.

[13] "I made my first fiberglass sculptures in 1994. But I have been working on sculptures only for three years. *Farbe* - with Heilman, Stockholder and Marcaccio - was the first time I came out of the wall with the monochrome colored-polystyrene-filled bags." Sébastien de Ganay (note, 30/04/04).

[14] What de Ganay most fundamentally has in common with McKracken is the sense of a "specific object", "things in themselves which refer solely to themselves, an art whose strength lies in its raw presence, imposing silence the better to act physically and intellectually on the onlooker." (John McCracken, press release, Galerie Almine Rech, Paris, 2000.)

[15] There's more to come in the way of art, too. De Ganay is already embarked on new angles (literally) as he explores the permutations and possibilities evolving out of this recent work. Here's an unrealized idea of his: take one of those steel donuts, scale it up to 10 meters and install it outdoors on a hill in such a way that it looks poised at the point of rolling down. Maybe the idea is so interesting that we don't even need to see the project realized, but who could possibly object?

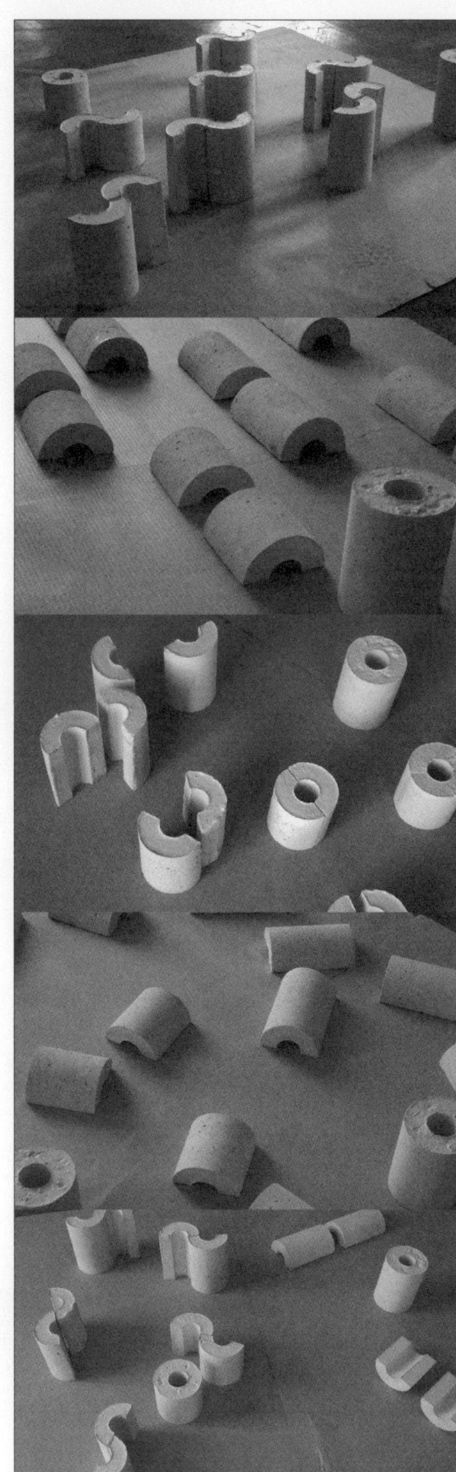

Concrete models of **Cylinders**, 2004.

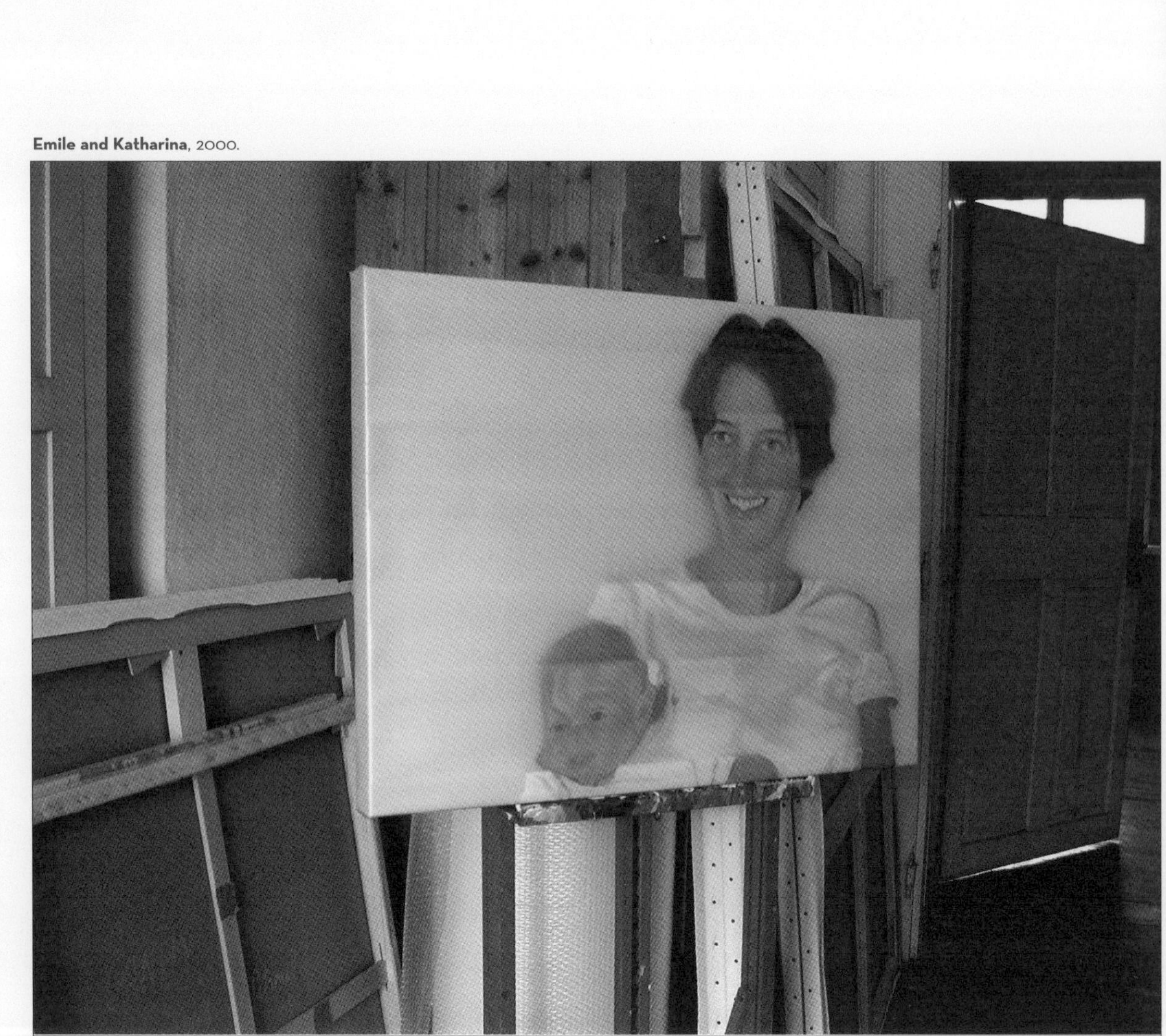

Emile and Katharina, 2000.

Dialog der Bilder

Ein Gespräch zwischen Sébastien de Ganay und Benedikt Ledebur

B.: Was an deinem weitgefächerten Werk auffällt, das modulare Skulpturen, Experimentieren mit Materialien und Analyse des Sehens wie des sozialen Feldes der Kunst miteinschließt, ist die zentrale Stellung der Malerei, und in ihr die des Portraits. Vielleicht willst du zu Beginn erzählen, wie du zum Malen gekommen bist und inwieweit die Malerei die Synthese deiner Beschäftigungen ausmacht?

S.: Es ist nicht nur richtig, dass die Malerei eine zentrale Stellung innerhalb meiner Arbeiten einnimmt, sie ist auch Ausgangspunkt aller meiner Beschäftigungen mit Installationen etc., die sich sozusagen von der Wand gelöst haben, um andere Räume für sich zu entdecken.

B.: Wann ungefähr hast du zu malen begonnen?

S.: Ich habe ziemlich spät mit dem Malen begonnen, so um 1984 herum, ich war 22 Jahre alt. Es war in New York. Moderne Malerei bedeutete für mich damals die amerikanische Malerei mit ihren Exponenten wie David Salle, Fischl, Basquiat oder Schnabel.

B.: Hattest Du auch persönlichen Kontakt zu jemandem von diesen Malern?

S.: Ja, aber das war eher zufällig, bei irgendwelchen

gesellschaftlichen Anlässen, und hatte keinen wirklichen Effekt auf meine eigene Produktion. Für diese war die Auseinandersetzung mit der früheren Generation, den Minimalisten wie Richard Serra, Ryman oder Donald Judd, viel wichtiger.

B.: Du hast gesagt, die Malerei sei der Ausgangspunkt gewesen, damals maltest du noch nicht auf gefaltetem Plastik, sondern in klassischer Manier auf Leinwand, was du übrigens ja auch nie ganz aufgegeben hast.

S.: Alles, womit ich mich einmal beschäftigt habe, kehrt eigentlich zyklisch irgendwann in meinen Arbeiten wieder. Obwohl ich mich als Maler verstand, meine Bilder also an die Wand hängte, habe ich damals sofort irgendwie versucht, die glatte Oberfläche der Farben aufzubrechen. Deswegen begann ich mit dem Falten. Für mich gab es damals keine gegenständliche Malerei. Das Portraitieren betrieb ich nur, um Geld zu verdienen.

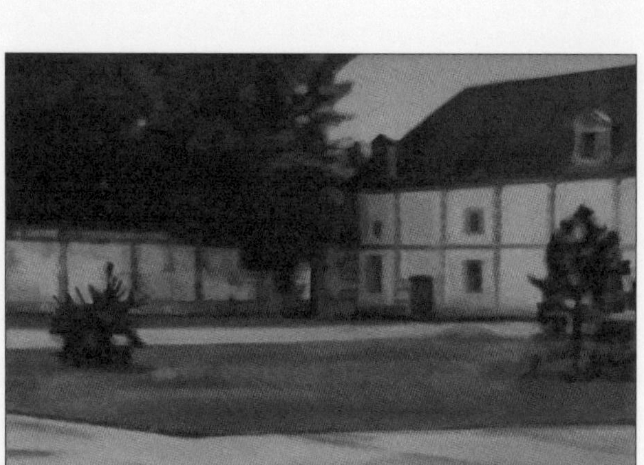

Miroir, Cour de ferme, 1996

B.: Aber jetzt ist doch die gegenständliche Malerei, das Portrait ein bedeutendes Element deiner Arbeiten. Wie ist es dazu gekommen?

S.: Ja, das stimmt, aber erst seit zwei Jahren, das heißt zwanzig Jahre später. Lange Zeit war das Portrait in der zeitgenössischen Kunstzene Tabu ...

B.: Aber es gab doch genug Künstler die Portraits anfertigten, man muss nicht an Warhol und Marilyn Monroe denken, was ist mit Francis Bacon, Lucien Freud, Hockney etc. Es gab doch genug anglo-amerikanische Künstler die dem Gegenständlichen verpflichtet geblieben sind. Gerade jetzt gibt es im Museum Moderner Kunst eine Ausstellung, die dem zeitgenössischen Portrait gewidmet ist.

S.: Du hast schon recht. Aber erstens hat mich die abstrakte Malerei mehr interessiert, und der Bereich gegenständliche Malerei schien mir irgendwie überbesetzt. Trotzdem scheint sich dieses Thema mit der Zeit auch bei mir durchgesetzt zu haben.

B.: Warte. Nur was das Portraitieren betrifft hast du erst vor zwei Jahren wieder damit begonnen, für die Grenze zwischen Abstraktion und Gegenständlich hast du dich ja durchgehend interessiert. Ich denke da an dein Experimentieren mit der Wahrnehmung, die Grenzen in den Bildern, deine *splitted images*, deine Spiegelbilder, die Straße nach Paris, plötzlich von einer Falte aufgebrochen, und wie deine gefalteten Portraits unter einer Plastikhaut ...

S.: Warum sprichst du von Grenze zwischen Abstraktion und Gegenständlich? Beide haben mich interessiert, beide Seiten haben gemeinsame Elemente in meiner Arbeit. Ich suche nach dem, was mir erlaubt, mich sowohl in dem einen wie dem anderen Bereich zu bewegen.

B.: Was heißt für dich Abstraktion? Geht sie vom Gegenständlichen aus? Ich denke da auch an dein Parallelarbeiten, das, während du zum Beispiel an den Portraits auf gefaltetem Plastik arbeitest, große Plastiksäcke mit bunten Würfeln produziert ...

S.: Die Plastiksäcke mit gefärbten Styroporwürfeln, sie erlauben mir, mit Räumen wie mit einem Stück Leinwand umzugehen, ich setze Farbpunkte, wie in der Münchner Ausstellung „Farbe", wo ich auch im Zweidimensionalen nur abstrakte Arbeiten auf gefaltetem Plastik gezeigt habe. Mein Arbeiten mit der etwas erweiterten Form des Tafelbildes gibt mir meistens das Gefühl, schon zu wissen, wie ich zu malen habe, der Plan ist schon da, während mir das Arbeiten im Raum ermöglicht, die kombinatorischen Aspekte des Arbeitens zu erkunden, die Möglichkeiten, zu arrangieren sind da fast unendlich. Das sind da weniger die Säcke oder Module, sondern die Möglichkeiten. In einer meiner nächsten Ausstellungen plane ich, etwa hundert Würfel in der Verpackung zu zeigen, wie ich sie von der Fabrik erhalten habe. Sie sind zusammen in durchsichtiges Plastik verpackt, sodass sie nicht bewegt werden können. Indem ich der Möglichkeit die Möglichkeit der Realisation raube, zeige ich dann quasi die reine Möglichkeit.

B.: Das wird dann zu den fast zu Ende gedachten, witzigen Installationen deiner konzeptuellen Arbeiten gehören. Dialektik ad absurdum.

S.: Du kannst aber immer noch das Plastik entfernen. Meine Arbeit kennt keine Berührungsängste. Manchmal ist es gut, den anderen das Risiko zu überlassen, sich zu amüsieren.

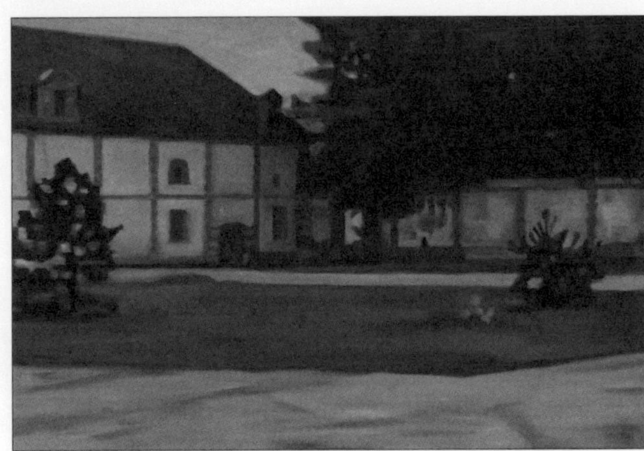

Miroir, Cour de ferme, 1996

B.: Oder nachzudenken. Kommt, wenn du nach deinen Modulen suchst, die Abstraktion für dich nach dem Gegenständlichen, ziehst du sie sozusagen aus deinen Erfahrungen die du beim nachahmenden oder nachziehenden Malen machst - du arbeitest ja mit der Projektion von Lichtbildern - und mit den dabei verwendeten Materialien, oder bedeutet für dich Abstraktion ein eigenes, gleichberechtigtes System, eine eigene Sprache mit selbständiger Grammatik, der du dich bedienst, ebenso wie du dich der Konventionen des Figurativen bedienst und diese schon im Bild aufbrichst? Schon im gegenständlichen Bild suchst du ja die Abstraktion oder zumindest eine ähnlich Fragestellung, mit deinen Inversen, den Auflösungen des Bildes in Pixel, den Falten usw.

S.: Für mich nährt das eine das andere. Die Mechanismen des einen wie des anderen liegen sich sehr nahe. Das ist eine zweifelhafte Frage, und vielleicht redet man da nur Unsinn. Ich arbeite nicht mit einer Doktrin, die meinem Malen vorhergeht, keine schon feststehende Ideologie oder Codierung geht meinem Arbeiten voraus. Ich habe eigentlich nie eine Analyse gemacht, warum bestimmte Beschäftigungen bei mir parallel laufen. Ich weiß aber, dass ich auf gewisse Prozesse zurückgreifen können muss, die auch von selbst wieder aufbrechen. Mechanismen, die sich aufdrängen, das Material strukturieren und dann auf die Arbeit rückwirken, auf meinen Stil. Es ist doch komisch, wie omnipräsent überall die philosophischen Zitate sind, in den Katalogen der Künstler, als ob philosophische Pläne den künstlerischen Werdegang bestimmen würden. Es sind fast Handicaps, Hickups, die mich da bewegen.

B.: Was bezeichnest du jetzt mit Hickups, sind das die Verfremdungen in deinen Arbeiten, die Falten, Spiegelungen und gröberen Strukturierungen?

S.: Ja, das sind diese ganzen mentalen Spiele. Du sprichst zum Beispiel vom Spiegel. Was mich interessieren würde ist, wie Bilder, die auf zwei Leinwänden wie Bild und Spiegelbild arrangiert sind, wie diese auf den Betrachter wirken. Mich interessiert die Wirkung dieser Art von Annullierung. Erinnerst du dich an das Bild vom Hof von Fleury, ein Meierhof, zweimal gemalt, einmal gespiegelt, das Hirn versucht diese Bilder miteinander zu versöhnen, der Dialog geschieht nicht mehr nur zwischen Betrachter und Bild, sondern die Bilder scheinen miteinander zu kommunizieren. Der Betrachter wird zum *spectateur d'un spectacle*, eines Dialogs der Bilder.

B.: Diese Analyse der Empfindungen, dieses ganz positivistische Interesse an der Wirkung auf die Psychologie des Betrachters, scheint also auch ein wesentlicher Aspekt zu sein, der sich in deinen Arbeiten niederschlägt. Sie macht aus den Produkten deiner Kunst ein Instrumentarium, das über das rein Ästhetische im üblichen Sinn hinausgeht, ein Instrumentarium der Erkenntnis. Du bist ja der erste Betrachter deiner Bilder, an dem du deine Experimente durchführst. Könnte man deine Säcke, deine geometrischen Elemente, Würfel, Zylinder, einfärbigen Aluminiumwände, kurz: deine Beschäftigung mit der Abstraktion also eher diesem Bereich des erkenntnistheoretisch interessierten Experimentierens zurechnen?

S.: Du vergisst das Interesse am Spiel. Das Spiel darin ist die Methode. Ich glaube, mich hat da auch sehr beeinflusst, meinen Kindern beim Spielen zuzusehen. Viele bildende Künstler kann man doch auch einfach als große Kinder betrachten, ein bisschen ist das mein Blick auf die ganze Kunstwelt. Nein, was mich wirklich interessiert ist, wenn ich mit meinen Installationen die Betrachter dazu animieren kann, mit den Gegenständen, die man ihnen anvertraut, ähnlich wie Kinder zu spielen und ihr Interesse an den Wirkungen zu wecken, die Lust an neuen Konstellationen, am elementaren Sehen, der Rekonstruktion, so wie ich sie bei mir selbst durch das Arbeiten zu wecken versuche. Für mich war an einem bestimmten Moment wichtig, wie ich den Betrachter dazu bekomme, zu intervenieren. Deshalb die einfachen Elemente wie Würfel. Ich habe 40 Säcke für die Galerie Häusler in München gemacht, und während der Austellung gab es dort jeden Tag eine neue Installation, sozusagen von den Besuchern hergestellt. Oder die Zylinder, die Halbzylinder, da gibt es soviele Kombinations-möglichkeiten, so wie man als Künstler immer irgendwohin will und nie ankommt, nie zufrieden ist, so soll auch der Betrachter dazu verführt werden, wie die Ratte in das Labyrinth dieser Kombinations-möglichkeiten zu geraten, *hands on art*, sie sind in den kreativen Prozess miteinbezogen.

B.: Es gibt also zwei Phasen des Experiments? Die eine ist die, wo du an dir selbst überprüfen kannst, sehe ich diese farbigen Mauern dreidimensional, wie wirkt das grelle Gelb neben dem Dunkelblau etc. Klassisches Wahrnehmungsexperiment also, wo du annehmen kannst, dass im Kopf des Betrachters das selbe wie in deinem Kopf vorgeht, die andere ist die wirkungspsychologisch unsichere, wie bekomme ich die Betrachter dazu, sich spielerisch mit den Arbeiten auseinanderzusetzen.

S.: Ja, wo du von den Mauern sprichst, die waren wirklich auch von einem speziellen Interesse geleitet. Es ist ein zweiter Reflexionsgrad, die Mauern die von wirklichen Mauern umschlossen sind, gleichzeitig haben sie doch auch eine offene Form. Da gibt es mehrere Ebenen, die mich an den Mauern interessieren, vor allem die kontradiktorischen Elemente, sie sind ja aus einem Material, von einer Farbe die man normalerweise nicht mit Mauern assoziiert, gleichzeitig haben sie viele Eigenschaften von Mauern, steht man ihnen direkt gegenüber, verlieren sie ihre Dreidimensionalität, sie wirken wie Bildzitate, wie monochrome Bilder, die sich in den Raum verselbständigt haben.

B.: So wie du die Oberfläche der Bilder faltest ist das also auch eine andere Art, den Bildbegriff zu erweitern. Das ist natürlich alles schon einmal geschehen in der Kunstgeschichte, sieht man einmal von deinem Abzielen auf die handgreifliche Interaktion zwischen Objekten und Betrachter ab. Ich sehe da zwei Formen der Annäherung bei dir, einerseits experimentierst du mit dir selbst und mit deiner Idee vom Betrachter, so baust du ein ziemlich isoliertes Experimentierfeld mit Objekten, Malweisen, Materialien um dich auf, alles was bei dir Analyse des Sehens etc. ausmacht gehört zu dieser Art Annäherung, andererseits fällt auf, dass du das, was andere zeitgenössische Künstlerinnen und Künstler fabrizieren, sehr aufmerksam mitverfolgst, auch als Sammler, dass du dich sehr stark über den unmittelbaren Kontext zeitgenössischer Kunst definierst. Wie siehst du dich bei dieser zweiten Form der künstlerischen Annäherung?

S.: Wie jeder andere Künstler, Verleger oder Sammler verfolge ich die Arbeit meiner Kollegen. Durch meine Künstlerfreunde entdecke ich verschiedenste Projekte und Wahrnehmungsmöglichkeiten, oft völlig konträr zu meiner eigenen Welt, die mir dafür aber andere, unerwartete Sphären eröffnen. Alles, was mich als künstlerisch tätigen Menschen und mein dadurch von mir definiertes Universum umgibt, wird automatisch absorbiert und verarbeitet. Worauf es aber schlussendlich ankommt, ist das Endprodukt dieses Prozesses.

B.: Natürlich haben diese mit dir befreundeten Künstler wieder ihre eigene Umgebung, und so ziehen sich langsam weitere Kreise und du wirst auch für das abstraktere Feld des Kunstbetriebes sensibilisiert, es wird zum Thema deiner Reflexionen beim Malen. Ich denke da zum Beispiel an deine letzten Bilder von Künstlern, wie das von Rudolf Polanszky, oder das, wo Erwin Wurm Franz West beim Weggehen beobachtet.

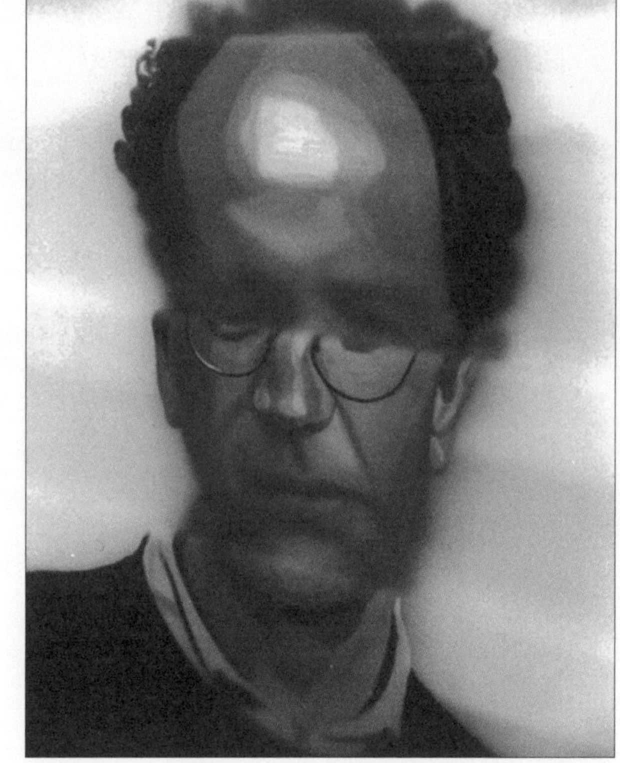

Detail of **Benedikt**, 2002

S.: Über dieses letzes Bild bin ich mir noch unsicher. Das sind Studien, und wer darauf dargestellt wird, ist für mich gar nicht so wichtig. Mich interessiert darin einfach die Bewegung, wie ein Mann einem anderen zusieht, wie er davongeht. Wer es ist, ist nur ein *surplus* das mich selbst amüsiert. Ich habe ja genauso anonyme Personen festgehalten. Aber als ich zum Beispiel dein Portrait gemacht habe, war für mich schon der Moment des Fotografierens interessant, weil natürlich ein Bekannter eine andere Pose mir gegenüber einnimmt, als jemand, den ich auf der Straße bitte, oder wie es in einem Schnapschuss zum Ausdruck kommt. Zum Beispiel die zwei alten Damen, die Arm in Arm über den Heldenplatz gehen, für mich ist das ein Bild, das sehr gelungen ist, weil es sich selbst entpersonalisiert, es steht plötzlich ganz symbolisch für das Altern vor mir. Umso länger ich überlege, umso mehr kommt mir vor, dass die Quelle des auf meinen Bildern Dargestellten nicht so wichtig ist. Es geht eher um die Transformation, den Akt des Malens.

B.: Ich erinnere mich da auch an Bilder, die du von Plakaten und alten Fotografien genommen hast.

S.: Das war, wie ich nach Österreich gekommen bin. Es waren gerade Wahlen, aus denen dann die neue Koalition, die in Europa soviel Probleme gehabt hat, hervorgegangen ist. Mich hat der Wahlkampf erstaunt, die Flut von Bildern, die strapazierte Bildkommunikation, und als die Galerie Steinek mit mir eine Ausstellung machen wollte, habe ich dann dieses Bildmaterial für mich genützt.

B.: Da war doch dieses in einem Zeitungsartikel besprochene Bild vom Kandidaten der freiheitlichen Partei, wie er sich über eine alte Frau beugt; es wurde analysiert und es zeigte sich, dass es nach irgend einer Methode der mentalen Programmierung arrangiert war, mir fällt jetzt der Name nicht ein. Du hast aber dann entdeckt, dass es ein Bild aus der Nazizeit gibt, das frappant der Konstellation ähnelt.

S.: Das Bild, das ich gefunden habe, stammte von der NSDAP 1937, und die Komposition wie das Sujet waren eigentlich ident mit dem im Wahlkampf 2000 verwendeten Bild. Die Wahl einer sehr alten Dame in Tracht, der auf sie blickende Sohn oder der lang verstorbene Gemahl, auch Erlösersymbolik, man kann da allerlei hineininterpretieren. Was mich interessierte, als ich die Ikonografie und die Mottos dieser fremdenfeindlichen Partei als Fremder, als Franzose in diesem Land entdeckte, war, wie man diese Bezüge aufdecken könnte. Ich habe also alte Fotobücher studiert, zum Beispiel das von August Sanders, der in den 30er Jahren die deutsche Bevölkerung fotografierte. Ich habe dann zwei Bilder von dem Band z.B. gewählt, einen Korpsstudent und das Bild eines Juden unter dem die Bezeichnung stand: "Junger Mann, verurteilt". Ich habe diese Bilder einander gegenübergestellt samt ihrem Negativ, also nur den Umriss, auf Plastik gemalt. Der Titel war dann *Heute ich, Morgen du*, ich habe das einmal irgendwo auf einem französischen Friedhof gelesen.

B.: Sonst kann man deine Kunst nicht wirklich politisch engagiert nennen.

S.: Damals war ich schon ziemlich schockiert und ich dachte, es sei dies der richtige Moment, mit den Bildern auch eine politische Aussage zu treffen. Sonst fühle ich mich als Betrachter, und sehe, was ich sehe. Gerade die letzten Arbeiten in Argentinien, du weißt schon, die *piqueteros* auf den zerschnittenen Baumstämmen. Es ist dort ein ziemlich harter sozialer Kampf im Gange. Es gibt viele Leute ohne Arbeit, ohne Sicherheit. Vor zwei Jahren, als die Wirtschaft dort zuammengekracht ist, gab es damals ziemlich grausame Zusammenstöße zwischen der Exekutive und den Demonstranten. Die *piqueteros* sieht man überall, sie blockieren die Hauptstraßen, die Arterien der Städte; jetzt muss die Regierung sie bezahlen, damit sie damit aufhören und eine Lebensgrundlage haben.

B.: Was hat dich daran für deine Darstellungen interessiert.

S.: Ich habe nicht aus der Realität gemalt, sondern Fotos genommen. Es waren Fotos zur Erinnerung an die Opfer, Demonstranten, die von der Polizei getötet worden sind. Die Bilder hatten eine Härte

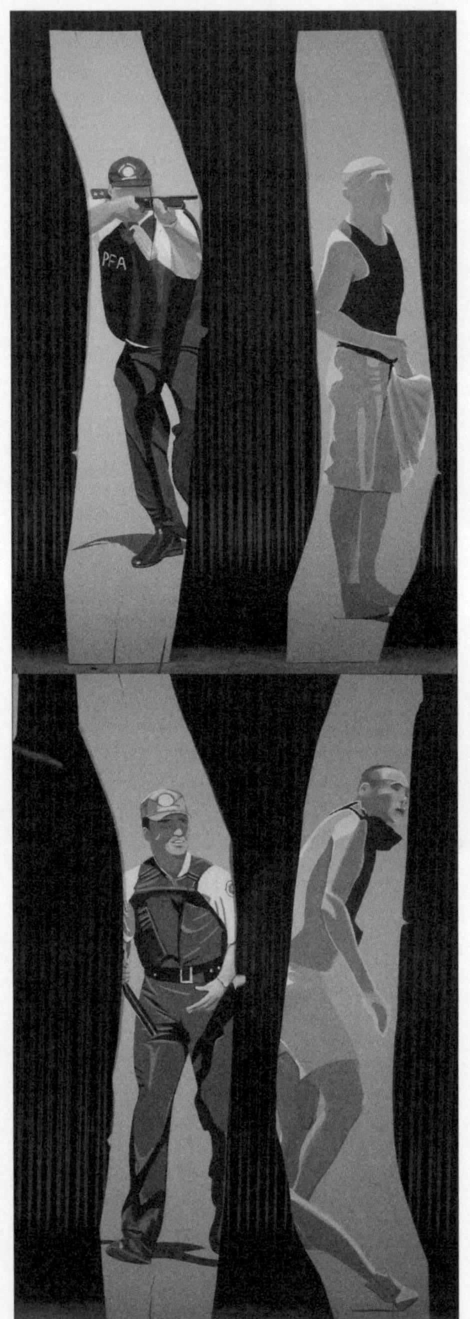

Details of **Piqueteros**, 2004

nicht nur z.B. wegen des Polizisten der in Richtung Fotograf zielt,
sondern weil die Bilder im Mittagslicht aufgenommen worden
sind, kleine Schatten und scharfe Umrisse, die mit dem vertikalen
Sonneneinstrahl diesen Todesbildern eine Klarheit gaben, die fast
schon wieder in Blendung kippt. Ich suche nicht die Ästhetisierung
der Gewalt, aber die Entsprechungen zwischen Motiv und Licht
haben mich bei diesen Bildern genauso interessiert wie
der soziale Aspekt.

B.: Warum behältst du in den Umrissen der Bretter, auf
denen diese Bilder gemalt sind, die ursprüngliche Form
des Baumes? Manche Bretter, die du dann für deine
Bauminstallationen benützt, sind sogar ohne figürliche
Darstellung, einheitlich weiß, grün, blau, rot, gelb
bemalt, und betonen diese natürliche Form.

S.: Zur Zeit benütze ich für meine Rauminstallationen
diese Grundfarben. Die Form des Baumes steht für
mich in enger Verbindung mit dem Menschlichen.
Die Bewegungen der dargestellten Menschen passen
sich der Bretterform an, das Holz ist nicht wie für
die Gemälde der Renaissance einfach eine praktisch
herstellbare Malunterlage, deren Herkunft, durch
die bearbeitete Oberfläche und die viereckige Form
versteckt, keine Rolle spielt. Vielleicht hat auch
unbewusst meine Begeisterung für die alten Begräbnis-
Portraits von Fayoum mitgespielt, die mit dem ganz
realistischen Kopfbild des portraitierten Verstorbenen
auf der Mumie das Gesicht ersetzen. Die Form der
Mumie ist, wie die Form des toten Baumes, ein
Hinweis auf etwas, das nicht mehr lebendig existiert.
Die Bauminstallationen sind dann wie eine weitere
Materialisierung dieses Hinweises, sowohl die Farben
wie auch das Aufgeschnittensein in Bretter markieren
die Künstlichkeit, die immer eine Bizarrerie oder
Fremdheit bedeutet. Das ermöglicht einem, in einen
anderen Kontext einzutreten, während die Möglichkeit,
aus den Brettern die Form des ganzen Baumes zu rekonstruieren,
die Erinnerung an das Abwesende, an das, was war, sehr konkret
werden lässt.

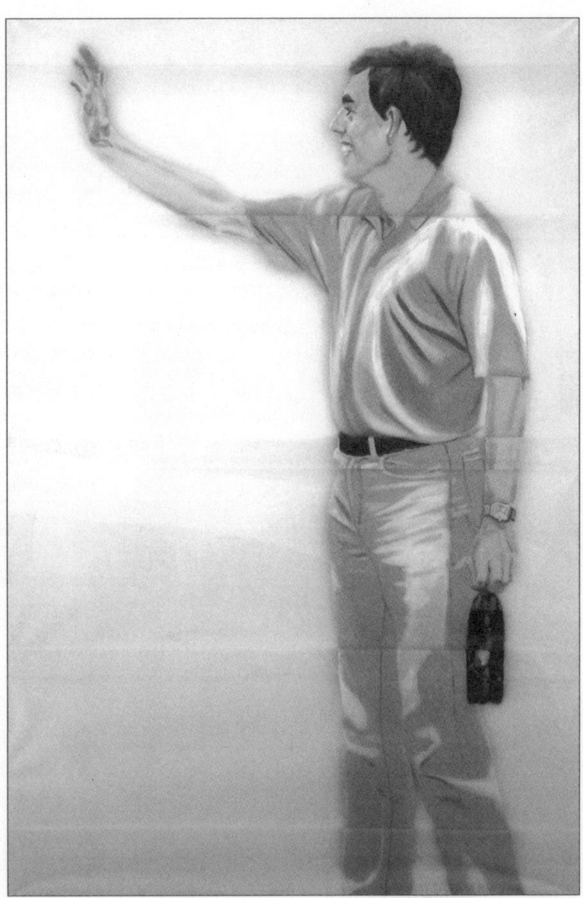

Edouard, 2004

B.: Hinsichtlich deines Experimentierens mit der Wahrnehmung,
bzw. Wirkung auf den Betrachter, hast du in letzter Zeit auch damit
begonnen, mit den Maßstäben zu spielen. Du bläst zum Beispiel
das Portrait eines sieben Jahre alten Kindes auf zwei Meter
auf und stellst daneben einen erwachsenen, beleibten Mann in
Lebensgröße. Nachdem du um deine Figuren meistens die Leinwand
leer lässt, und ihnen so der räumliche Kontext abhanden kommt,
ist die Irritation beim Betrachter durch die unterschiedlichen
Maßstäbe noch größer. Was ist für dich die Funktion dieser Irritation
und was ist der ästhetische Gewinn dabei, oder kann man sagen,
dass das Experimentieren im Ästhetischen auch auf Kosten dieses
Gewinns gehen kann.

S.: Ich habe wie oft bei meinen Produktionen durch Zufall damit
begonnen. Oft sieht man ja etwas nur wegen einer überraschenden
Konstellation. Ein junger Mann wollte unbedingt, dass ich ein
Portrait von ihm male. Bis seine Eltern nachgaben und ich schließlich
ein besonders großes Portrait, außerhalb meiner gewohnten
Normen malte. Als es fertig war, und an der Wand hing, sah es ganz

normal aus, sobald ich es aber neben das Portrait von Polanszky hängte, merkte ich plötzlich den Effekt, den die unterschiedlichen Maßstäbe auf mich hatten. Während das Nebeneinander der gespiegelten Bilder, von dem wir schon sprachen, so etwas wie eine Annullierung provozierten, hatte es hier einen ganz anderen Effekt, nämlich den eines räumlichen Paradoxons; das Bild des Mädchens, das in seiner Isolation ganz friedlich wirkte, hatte plötzlich etwas lebendigeres, fast agressives neben dem Mann in Lebensgröße. Beim Betrachten hatte ich auch das Gefühl eines eigenartigen Verzögerungseffektes, der vielleicht dadurch entsteht, dass das Hirn einen adäquaten Raum für die beiden Bilder zu konstruieren versucht und daran scheitert. Man versucht beim Betrachten solcher Gegensätze ganz unwillkürlich, und anders, als wenn man nur ein Bild betrachtet, sich auch selbst in einen räumlichen Bezug zu den Bildern zu setzen, ja das Bild in Überlebensgröße und die eigene Lebensgröße oder die eines Betrachters genügt eigentlich schon, dieser Kippeffekt braucht kein zweites Bild, damit man plötztlich wie *Alice in Wonderland* die Raumlogik gestört findet. Die Richtung dieses Sehens und In-räumliche-Beziehung-Setzens ist fast so etwas wie die Dekonstruktion illusionärer Räume.

B.: Das, was du als Maler, innerhalb des Bildraumes durch die isolierten Figuren und mit den Bildern im Ausstellungsraum versuchst, und hier ansprichst, erinnert mich ein bisschen an das, was James Turell mithilfe von Licht, Laserstrahlen und optischen Hilfsmitteln auf viel konzeptuellere Art mit dem Betrachter versucht: ein Bewusstmachen räumlichen Sehens. Es gab eine Ausstellung im Museum für Angewande Kunst in Wien, die mich damals sehr beeindruckt hat, wo er den Besucher mit einem in grelles Licht getauchten Raum konfrontierte, in dem die begrenzenden Kanten nicht mehr sichtbar waren, oder mit anderen dunklen Räumen, wo die Laserstrahlen die Kanten simulierten, nur eine fehlte und man sich dieses langsamen Konstruierens von Raum bewusst wurde. Interessiert dich auch dieser rein mentale Aspekt bei deinem Umgang mit deinen Bildern und Objekten?

S.: Natürlich liegt meine Suche am ganz anderen Ende des künstlerischen Spektrums, und steht in der Tradition der Malerei. Dieses Experimentieren mit den mentalen Aspekten des Sehens macht mir Spaß, aber das was in der konzeptuellen Kunst oft viel strenger untersucht wird und untersuchbar ist, ist bei mir nur ein Aspekt der Synthese die ich vor Augen habe, der Witz und die Allusion, die soziale Bedingtheit, die malerischen Techniken und Möglichkeiten, das schon vorgefundene Bildmaterial, all das, was bei mir sonst noch zum Thema wird, hat bei mir genauso hohen Stellenwert. Ich sehe zwar, dass die Malerei im Kunstbetrieb eine gewisse Renaissance erlebt, aber oft kommt mir vor, dieses lustige Drauflosmalen ist nur eine Reaktion auf die Moderne und keine Integration des Erreichten. Es ist fast so, also ob diese ganzen Dekonstruktionen und Experimente umsonst gewesen seien. Mich interessiert bei meinem Arbeiten die Reflexion im Machen und Sehen, die möglichen Verbindungen zwischen den sensuellen Aspekten, der Selbstbeobachtung und ihrem rationalen Verarbeiten. Aber natürlich hat das alles für das Werk nur soweit Relevanz, wie es sich ins Sinnliche, in eine überzeugende Komposition rückübersetzt.

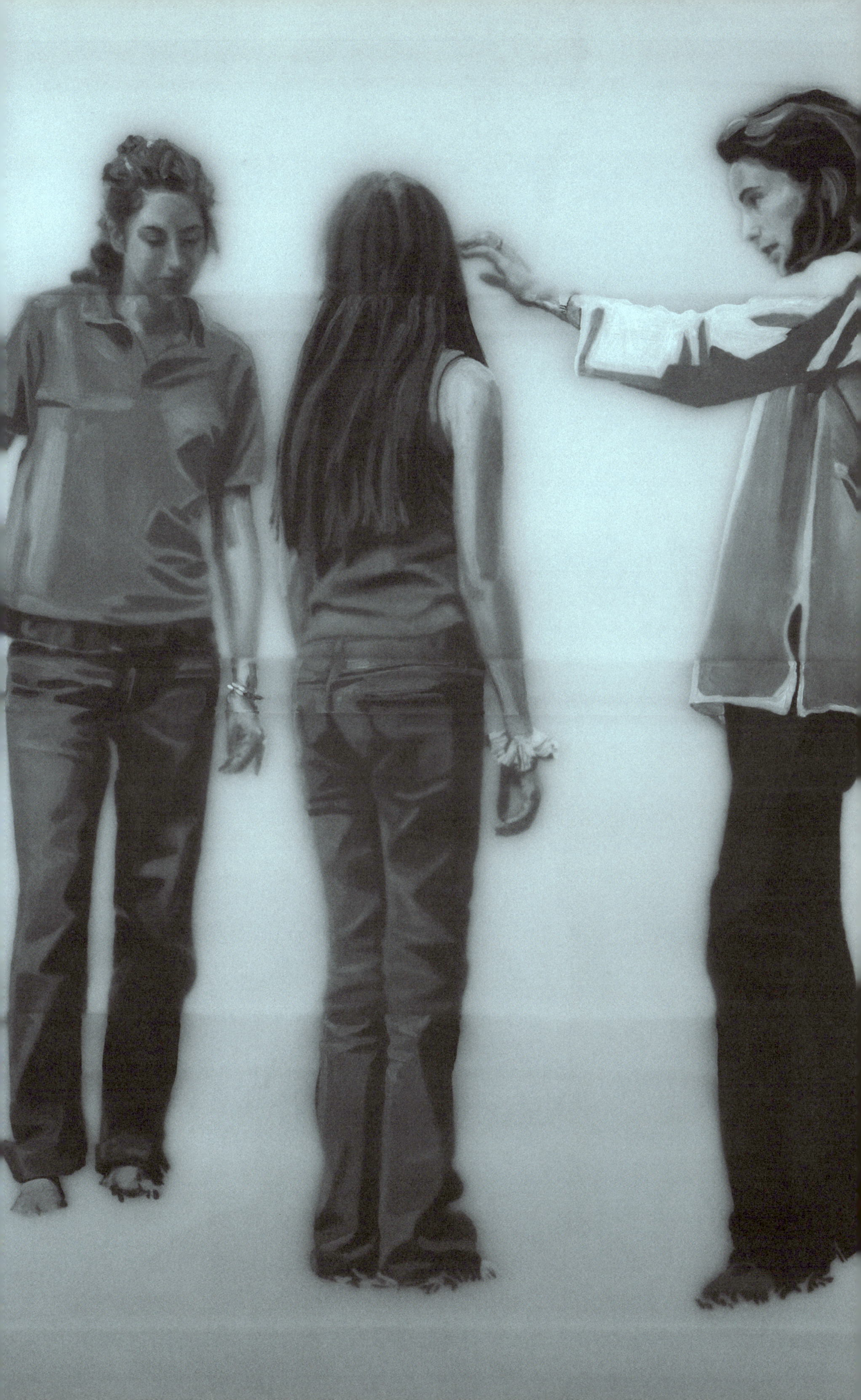

Ferdinand, 2002.

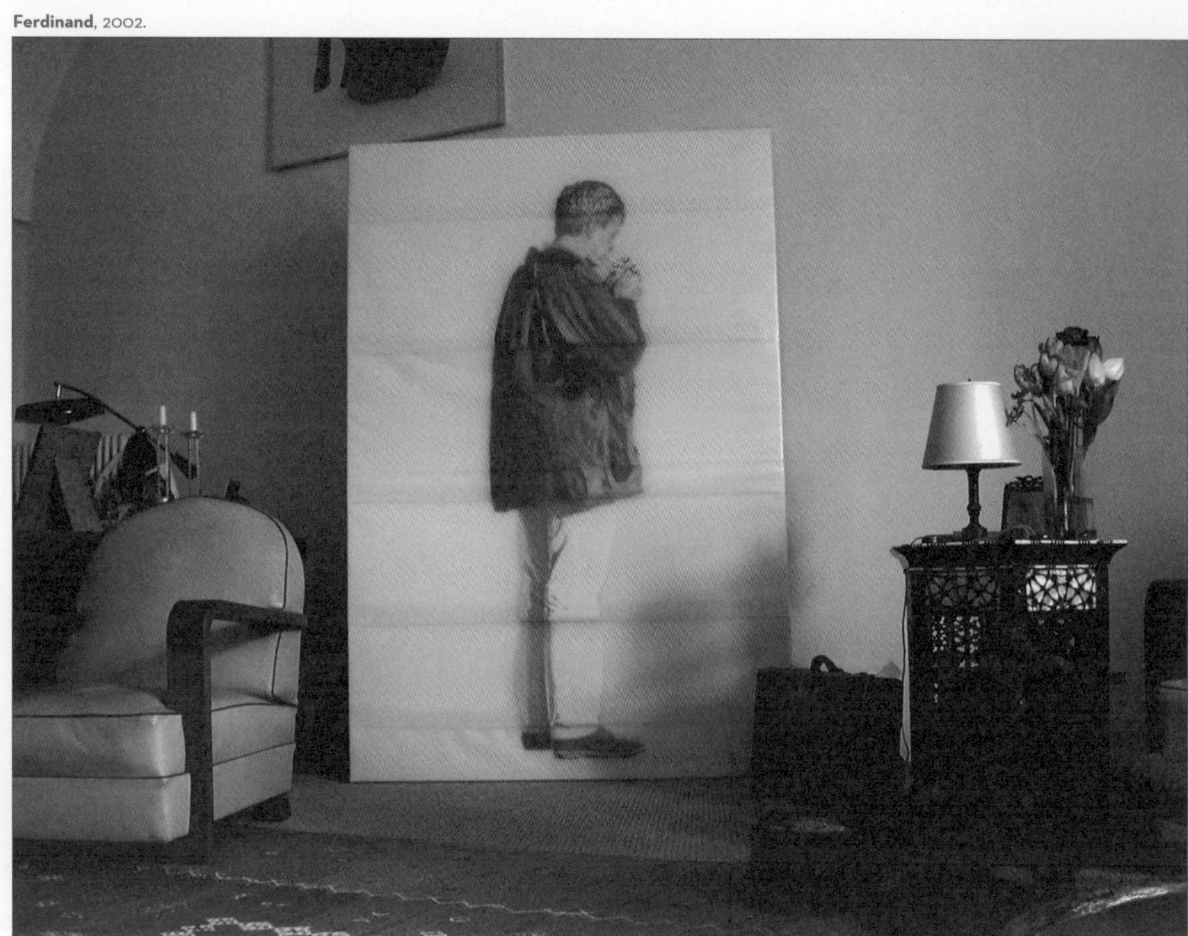

Dialog of Images

Conversation Between Sébastien de Ganay and Benedikt Ledebur

B.: Your wide-ranging work includes modular sculptures, experiments with materials, as well as analyses of seeing and the social field of art. What strikes me is the central position occupied by painting, and the focus of painting on portraits. So, to begin with, maybe you would like to recount how you arrived at emphasizing painting and to which extent painting stands as a synthesis of your occupations?

S.: It's not only true that painting occupies a central position within my works, it is also the point of departure for all my attempts at installations etc. that have, as it were, detached themselves from the wall in order to discover new spaces for themselves.

B.: About when did you get involved in painting?

S.: I took up painting rather late, somewhere around 1984, when I was about 22. I was in New York at the time and my understanding of modern painting derived from American painting whose exponents included David Salle, Fischl, Basquiat, or Schnabel.

B.: Did you make personal contacts with any of these artists?

S.: Yes, but mostly by chance; I got to meet them at social events, but that hardly had any genuine influence on my own production.

Being exposed to artists from the earlier generation, to minimalists such as Richard Serra, Ryman, or Donald Judd, was far more important.

B.: You say that painting was your point of departure. Back then, you were not painting on folded plastic but worked on canvas in a classic manner, something which, by the way, you have never entirely given up.

S.: Everything I have dealt with at some point actually recurs in my works in a cyclical movement. Even though I considered myself to be a painter and hung my pictures on the wall, I immediately tried to break open the slick surface of colors. This is why I came up with the folding process. At the time, representational painting had no validity for me at all. Portraits were just a means for me to make some money.

B.: But nowadays, representational painting and portraits are a chief element of your work. Now, how did that come about?

S.: Yes, that's true, but only for the last two years, twenty years down the road, that is. For a long time, portraits was a taboo subject among contemporary artists...

B.: But there were plenty of artists who did portraits; one doesn't need to cite Warhol and his Marilyn Monroe, what about Francis Bacon, Lucien Freud, Hockney etc.? And then there was also a host of Anglo-American artists who kept up their commitment to representational imagery. Right now, the Museum of Modern Art runs an exhibit dedicated to present-day portraits.

S.: Sure, but first of all I was more interested in abstract painting and the field of representational painting appeared to me as somehow too crowded. Over time, of course, this theme apparently did strike a chord with me, too.

B.: Wait. With regard to portraits, you only picked up on the matter again two years ago; however, the limits separating abstract and representational painting have been a point of reference for you all along. What I'm thinking of are your experiments with perceptions, the borders worked into your imagery, your "splitted image", your mirror images, the road to Paris, all of a sudden furrowed with a crease, and how your folded portraits underneath a skin of plastic...

S.: Why are you talking about a line between abstract and representational? Both have been interesting to me, both sides have common elements, in my work. I am looking for something that will allow me to move on both sides of this divide.

B.: What is your idea of abstraction? Does it start from the representational? What I also have in mind here are your parallel works, meaning that while you are working on a portrait on folded plastic, you are filling large plastic bags with multicolored cubes at the same time...

S.: The plastic bags with colored styrofoam cubes, they enable me to deal with spaces such as a piece of canvas; I create color fields within a volume, as I did at the "Farbe" exhibit in Munich where my pictures, too, only showed color on folded plastic. Working with the

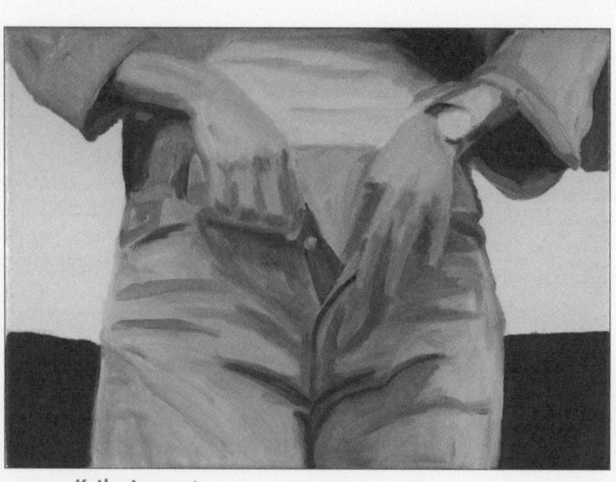

Katharina, 1996

somewhat extended form of the panel painting mostly gives me a feeling of already knowing how I will have to go about the painting process; the plan is there from the start, whereas working in open spaces lets me explore the combinatorial aspects of my work where the number of possible arrangements is almost endless. This is not so much about bags or modules but about possibilities. At one of my upcoming exhibits, I am planning on showing about one hundred cubes inside their wrapping, just as I picked them up at the factory. They are stacked inside transparent plastic film so that they cannot be moved. By disabling the possibility of any possibility becoming real, I end up displaying, as it were, the pure possibility itself.

B.: This will rank as one of the witty installations of your conceptual work that are almost thought through to the end. Dialectics reduced to absurdity.

S.: But you can always remove the plastic film. My work is never scared at the idea of contact. Sometimes it's good to leave the risk of enjoying themselves to others.

B.: Or of giving it some thought. When you are on the lookout for your modules, does abstraction follow the representational, do you extract it, so to speak, from your experiences gained from brush strokes that imitate and retrace -- you actually use projections of photographs -- and from the materials you use? Or do you conceive of abstraction as a separate, equally valid system, a language of its own with an independent grammar that you turn to in the same way as you make use of the conventions of figurative art that you already break open in the picture? Already with representational imagery, you are trying to achieve abstraction, or at least a similar way of putting the question, with your inversions, resolving of images into pixels, creases etc.

S.: For me, each of the two feeds on the other. The mechanisms of either of the two are not far apart. This is a dubious question, and it could well be that it amounts to talking nonsense. I do not work on the basis of any doctrine that precedes my painting, no fixed ideology or coding is antecedent to my work. I have actually never made any analysis of why I engage in certain occupations simultaneously. But I know that I need to be able to fall back on specific processes that also set off again of their accord. Mechanisms that suggest themselves, restructuring my materials and retroactively influencing my work and style. Isn't it strange so see how omnipresent philosophical quotations are everywhere, in artist's catalogs, as if philosophical schemes were driving artistic development. With me, its almost handicaps, hiccups that get me going.

B.: What is it that you mean by hiccups, is it the alienation effects in your works, the creases, mirroring and courser structures?

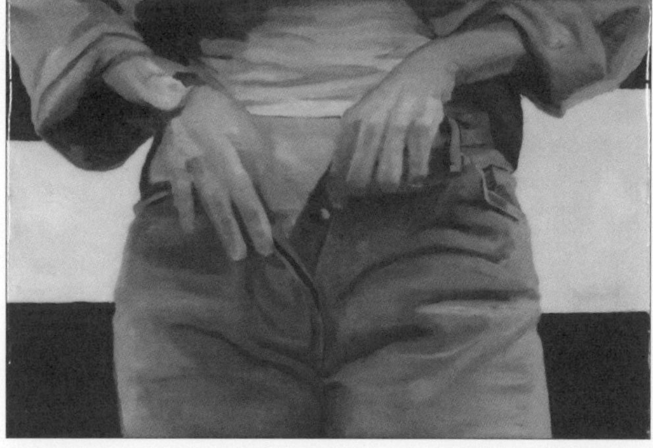

Katharina, 1996

S.: Yes, all the mental games. You're talking about mirrors, for example. What I'd like to know is what impressions onlookers are left with when two images on canvasses are arranged in the manner of an image and its reflection. I'm interested in the effect of this kind of annulment. Do you remember the picture of the Fleury farm, a farmhouse painted twice, one mirror image; the brain tries to reconcile these two pictures. The Dialog not only involves the viewer and the image, but the two images seem to communicate with each other. The observer turns into a "spectateur d'un spectacle", of a dialog of images.

B.: This analysis of sensory perceptions and emotions, this wholly positivistic interest in the effect on the psychology of viewers, that, too, appears as a chief aspect reflected in your work. It's a procedure that turns the products of your art into a set of instruments that goes beyond the purely aesthetic as it is generally conceived of. They're cognitive instruments. Now, given the fact that you yourself are the first viewer of your pictures who is subjected to your experiments, couldn't we say that your bags, geometric elements, cubes, cylinders, monochrome aluminum walls -- in short: your employment of abstraction, shouldn't this rather be counted as an epistemological experiment?

S.: Don't forget the interesting part of the game. The name of the game is the method. I guess that watching my kids play has had great influence on me. Many visual artists can simply be labeled as grown children, and this, to some extent, tells you what my view

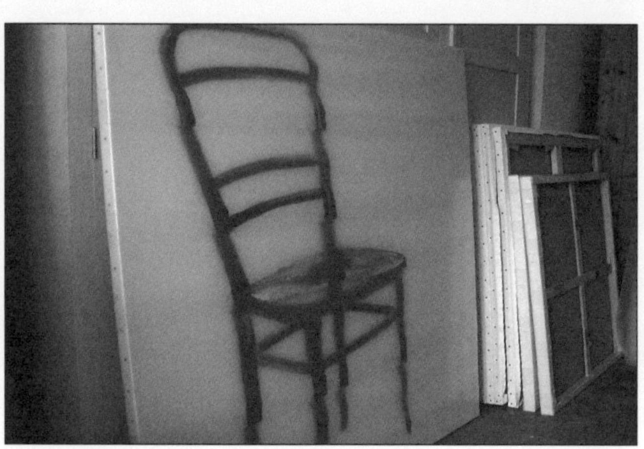

Chair 1, 2004

of the whole art world is all about. No, what I am really curious about is to encourage onlookers to take my installations to be something that is placed in their hands, as you would give children objects to play with. I'm trying to arouse curiosity about the effects, get people to have fun in creating new constellations and engage in a basic form of seeing, reconstruction, just as I try to awaken these faculties with myself through my work. There was a point where it became important to me to find out how I could get observers to intervene. Hence the simple elements such as cubes. I made 40 bags for Galerie Häusler in Munich, and in the course of the exhibit you could witness a new installation there every day, so to speak, that was created by visitors. Or take the cylinders, the half-cylinders, there are so many possible combinations, and just as the artist is always headed for something he will never arrive at, just as he or she will never be satisfied, the viewer, too, like a rat should be lured into this labyrinth of endless possible combinations. It's a "hands on art", they are included and get involved with the creative process.

B.: Does that mean there are two phases of the experiment? First, you go ahead and check to see whether these colored walls have a three-dimensional effect, or how a bright yellow will look beside a dark blue etc. Therefore, a classic perceptual experiment where you can assume that what takes place inside your own head also will take place inside the mind of the observer. Second, there is an uncertain response theory about how viewers can be enticed to adopt a playful attitude towards your work.

S.: Well, yes. You've mentioned these walls, and they originated from a specific train of thought. It's a second level of reflection, these walls that are enclosed by true walls, which at the same time have an open form. There are several levels to these "walls" that are interesting to me, especially the contradictory elements, meaning they are made of materials commonly not associated with walls, while also showing a number of characteristics found on real walls. Looking at them from up close, they loose their three-dimensional appearance; they strike you as being pictorial quotations, monochrome images that have become independent in space.

B.: The way you fold the surface of images, therefore, is an attempt at extending the concept of the picture. Of course, all this has already been done in the history of art, apart from your aiming at physical interaction between objects and viewers. I have a hunch that you employ two methods of approximation; on the one hand, you subject yourself and your notion of the viewer to experiments, thereby creating a fairly isolated experimental field of objects, painting styles, and materials around you. Everything that is related to your analysis of seeing etc. is part of this type of approximation. On the other hand, you are obviously closely watching what other contemporary artists concoct -- this is also true for you as a collector -- and that you strongly define yourself in relation to the immediate context of contemporary art. What is your own understanding of this, your second mode of artistic approximation?

S.: As any other artist, publisher or collector I am keeping track of what my peers are doing. Through my artists friends I have the privilege of discovering lots of projects and sensibilities totally remote from mine but yet terribly mind broadening. However, once an artist is on his track, defining his universe, anything relating to it is absorbed and digested. What counts is what comes out of it.

B.: Of course, artist acquaintances of yours in turn have their own immediate social surroundings, and so gradually you reach out further and further, thus increasing sensitivity towards the more abstract field of the art world; this subject matter is then reflected in your paintings. I'm thinking of your recent portraits of artists, for example of Rudolf Polanszky or Erwin Wurm watching Franz West.

S.: I'm still not really sure about this picture. These are all studies, and it doesn't matter all that much who is in the picture. I simply focus on the movement, the way one man watches another as he is leaving. Who it is that appears in the image, that's just a surplus value, and simply amusing to me. Mind you, I have captured anonymous persons in the same manner. But when I did your portrait, for example, the moment of taking the picture itself was interesting to me, because, naturally, someone I know personally will take up a different pose than people I approach on the street, and a snapshot again will express something different. For instance, the two elder ladies, walking arm in arm across Vienna's Heldenplatz Square. To me, the picture has turned out well; it depersonalizes itself, it's there in front of me, suddenly becoming a symbol of growing old. The more I think about it, the more I realize that the sources of the people and objects I show is of minor importance. I'm more concerned with transformation, the act of painting.

B.: This reminds me of pictures of yours that were taken from posters and old photographs.

S.: I did these when I came to Austria. There was an election at the time, the one eventually leading to the new coalition that was faced with so many problems throughout Europe. I was amazed at the election campaigns, the flood of images, the overtaxed communication of imagery, and when Galerie Steinek wanted to do an exhibition with me, I used this material.

B.: There was a picture that had been subject of a newspaper article. It showed the candidate of the Freedom Party bowing down to an old woman; an analysis showed it to be arranged in accordance with some method of mental programming, I can't think of the name right now. But you later discovered that there was a picture from the Nazi era that bears a striking resemblance to this constellation.

S.: The NSDAP picture I came across was from 1937, and the composition as well as the subject were practically identical with the one used in the 2000 campaign. The choice of an old lady clad in traditional attire, her son or long-deceased husband looking down on her, also this symbolism of the Savior, there are a lot of things one can read into this. Being French and a foreigner in this country, I was curious to uncover the references when I was faced with the iconography and the mottos used by this xenophobic

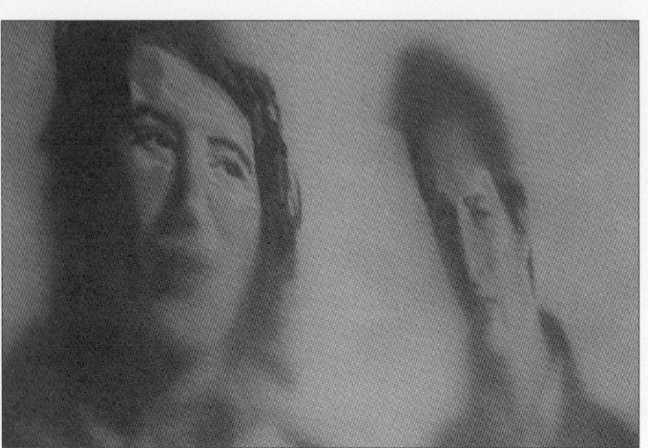

Detail of **Selina and Uriel,** 2002

party. Hence, I began to study old photo volumes, for example the one by August Sanders with his pictures of the German population in the thirties. I picked two images from this book, for instance, one depicting a student member of a dueling fraternity and one of a Jew whose caption read: "Young man, persecuted". I juxtaposed these two photos including the negatives, only the outlines, that is, and painted them on plastic. The title read "Me Today, and You Tomorrow", that's a line I saw once on a French graveyard.

B.: Aside from this, your art does not really carry any political content.

S.: I was quite shocked at the time and thought that this was the right moment to also convey a political message with these pictures. Other than that, I consider myself to be an observer and see whatever I see. Especially with my most recent work done in Argentina, you know, the *Piqueteros* on these cut-up logs; its a really tough social struggle going on there these days. There are so many people without jobs, without security. Two years ago, when the economy collapsed, they had these rather cruel clashes between police forces and demonstrators. You see the *Piqueteros* everywhere, they block the main roads, the city arteries, and the government is now paying them trying to stop their actions and provide them with a means of survival.

B.: What was it that attracted your attention and made you include it in your portrayal?

S.: I didn't paint from reality but took photos. These were pictures commemorating victims, demonstrators killed by police forces. The images were tough, not only because of police aiming a gun at the photographer, but on account of the noon light at the time the pictures were taken that created small shadows and sharp outlines. The vertical sunlight bathed these pictures of death in clarity that borders on a blinding glare. I am not into the aesthetics of violence, but with these images, the corresponding motifs and lighting were just as interesting to me as the social aspect.

B.: Why do you keep the unworked outlines of the wooden boards on which you did these paintings? We see the original form of the tree and some of the boards you used in your tree installations are even devoid of figurative elements, painted uniformly white, green, blue, yellow, emphasizing a natural form.

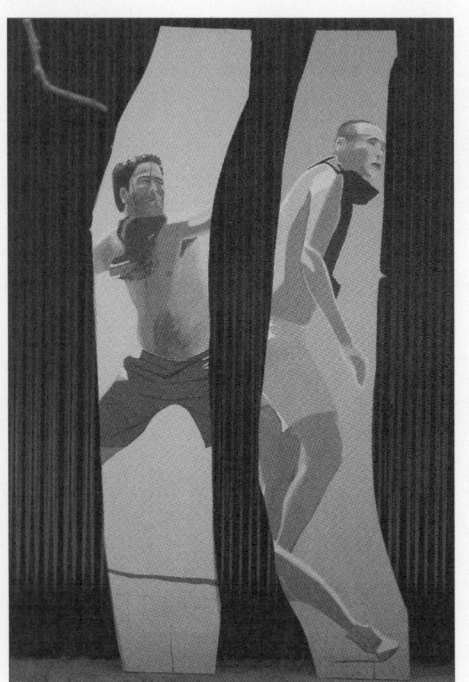

Details of **Piqueteros,** 2004

S.: At the moment I use these basic colors for my space installations. The form of the tree, to me, is closely connected with human nature. The movement of the people depicted here match with the shape of the boards. Wood is not simply something to paint on that is conveniently available as with Renaissance panel paintings where the worked surface and rectangular form hide its origins and renders it unimportant. It could well be that my fascination with the ancient burial portraits of Fayoum played a role in this. There, a wholly realistic portrait of the deceased person's head replaces the face of the mummy. The mummy's shape, just as the shape of the dead tree, points to something that does not exist alive any longer. The tree installations, then, are a material reference; the colors and the cut-open wood mark the artificiality -- which always amounts to something bizarre and alien -- that enables me to enter into a different context, while the possibility of reconstructing the whole tree from the boards, the memory of the absent, of that which was, becomes highly tangible.

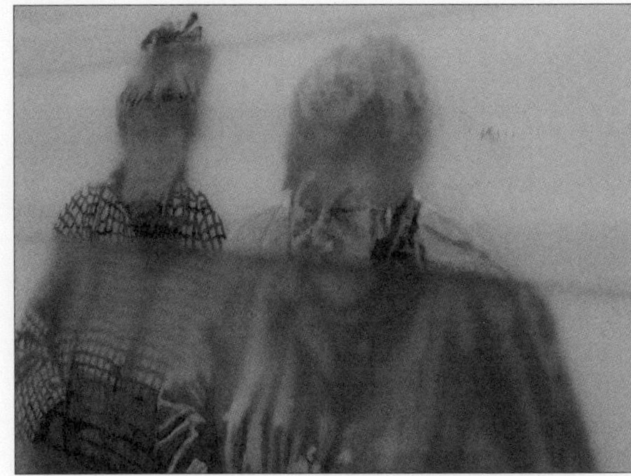

Detail of **Old Ladies,** 2002

B.: As to your perceptual experiments, which focus on the effect felt by observers, you have recently begun to play with the scaling of dimensions. As an example, there was a seven-year-old blown-up to a size of two meters, and you placed a life-sized, grown-up, stout man at its side. After mostly leaving the canvas surrounding your figures empty, by which they loose their spatial context, the irritation caused with viewers is now increased through the application of different scales. What function is it that you attribute to this irritation, what's the aesthetic gain here; or could we say that aesthetic experiments can be conducted at the expense of aesthetic gain?

S.: As with so many of my productions, I began working on this one by chance. Frequently, one turns one's eyes to something for the sake of surprising constellations. There was a young man who absolutely wanted me to do a portrait of him. His parents eventually yielded to his wish. I ended up doing a large-scale portrait way beyond my usual standard sizes. When it was done and hung on the wall, it looked perfectly normal, but when I hung it beside the portrait of Polanszky, I suddenly realized the effect I felt from varying scales. While the juxtaposition of mirrored images that we talked about earlier provoked a kind of annulment, I was faced with a completely different impression of a spatial paradox. The picture of the girl that looked perfectly peaceful in her isolation suddenly assumed a lively, almost aggressive appearance when contrasted with the life-sized man. When I looked at it, I had the strange sensation of a delaying effect that maybe arises from the brain's inability to construct an adequate space for both images. When observing such contrasts, we automatically -- and different than we would when viewing a single image – come up with a spatial relationship to ourselves. Actually, a single larger-than-life image will do to cause a tilting effect. Like Alice in Wonderland , our space logic is disturbed, and the direction of this act of seeing and creating spatial relationships is almost a deconstruction of illusionary spaces.

B.: What you try to accomplish as a painter by means of isolated figures within the space of the image and of pictures inside the exhibition space, and also what you have just touched upon, this reminds me of James Turell's strongly conceptual works. He used light, laser beams and visual aids to achieve a comparable effect with viewers: awareness of spatial visual perception. At the time, I was very impressed with his exhibition at the Museum of Applied Arts in Vienna. He confronted visitors with a room immersed in dazzlingly bright light where edges were no longer visible. There were also dark rooms with laser beams simulating edges, only one was missing, and the gradual construction of space became palpable. Are you interested in this purely mental aspect when you deal with your images and objects?

S.: Of course, my pursuit is really conducted at the opposite end of the artistic spectrum and is rooted in the tradition of painting. All these experiments concerning the mental aspects of seeing are simply great fun, but the things that can be and are frequently investigated more rigorously by conceptual art, all that is just one aspect of a synthesis I have in mind. The laughs and allusions, the social conditionality, the painting techniques and possibilities, the prefabricated imagery I come across, along with all the other topics that surface in my work play an equally important role. Even though I see that painting, to a certain extent, is going through a period of revival, to my mind this manner of happily painting away is just a reaction to modern art and not an integration of what has been achieved. It almost seems as if all these deconstructions and experiments have been staged in vain. With my work, I am interested in reflecting, doing, and seeing, the potential connections between sensory aspects, introspection and its assimilation by rational thought. But of course this is only relevant to the work in so far as it translates back into convincing compositions on the sensory level.

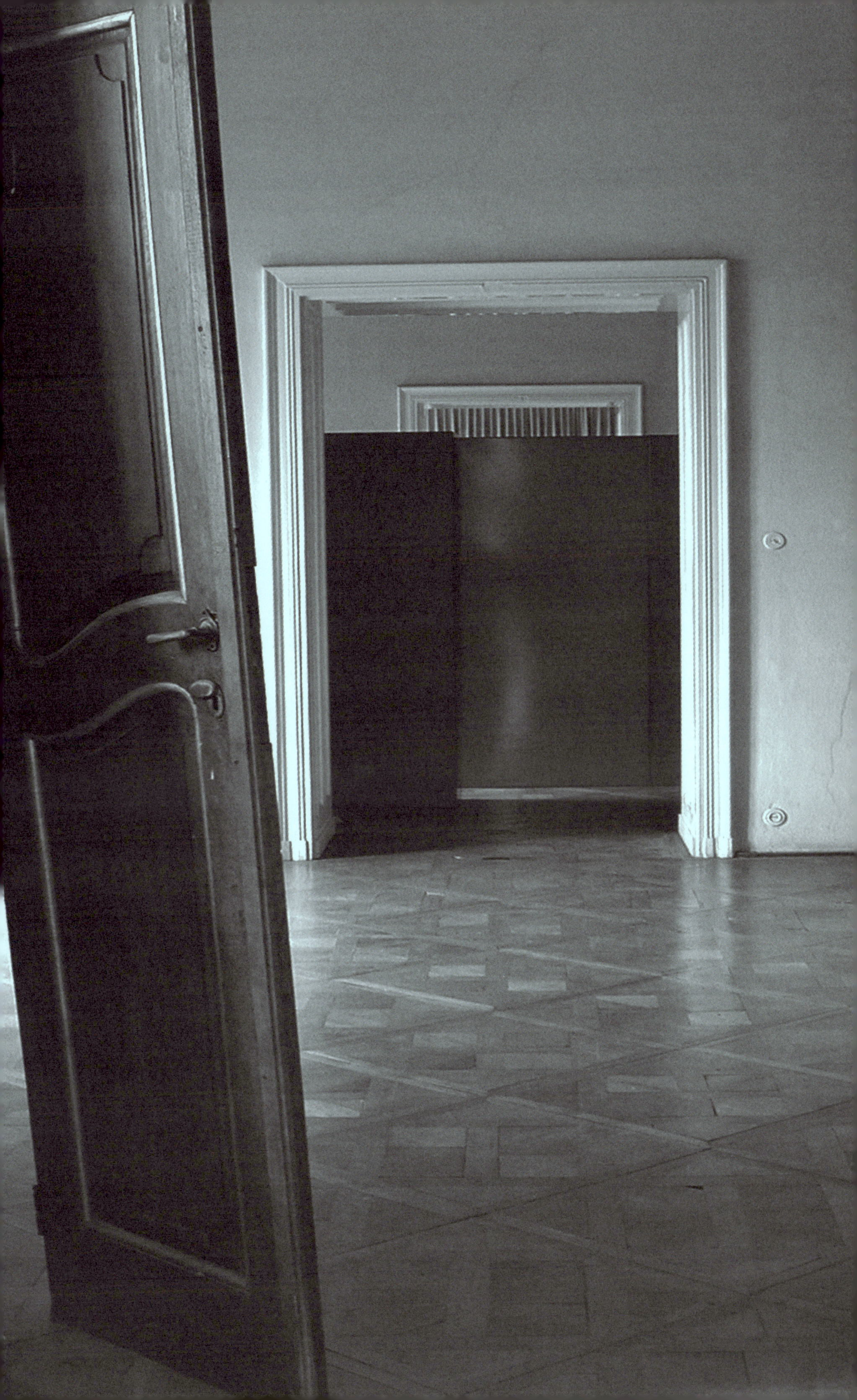

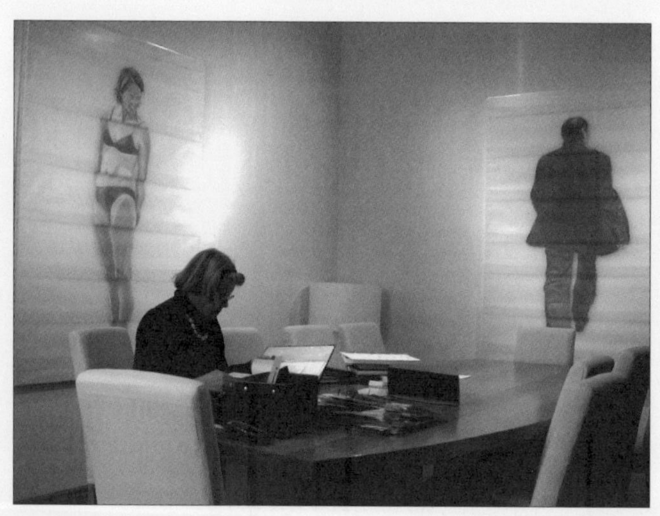

Dear Sébastien,

Sometimes reality - my daily reality - leads me directly into a movie or a piece
of art which I have seen. It's a certain picture or the movement of a person
or her face that makes the connection. It can be the whole image that comes
to me - or more often just a person in a non-existant background such as a
cutout- like your series of portraits of friends.
The girl sitting with the tender gesture or the woman standing - both persons
are painted from behind. The face is not important as in some memories
where we only see a depersonalized image of the world.

The images change between focused and unfocused parts - also like in
our memory and they seem to levitate in the empty space of the painting.
But they are not like cutouts or collages, because your persons are very
connected to the ground through the way how you fold the "canvas".
A lying women is even kind of melting into the "canvas"
And then - this I realized much later and not in front of your paintings - all
these persons have no shadows.

All this creates a certain disaster to me, but this is exactly what connects your
work to the films of David Lynch and the Coen brothers.
Art and Disaster. The simple story of the beginning gets more and more
complex like the traps of one of your fellow countryman who was perhaps the
first to write -that we can be sure that we see all the things we believe to see.
But we cannot be sure that when we kiss our kids goodnight that they exist
- although we see them.
This leads me to your wall pieces - and here again the movies- we get very
much conscious about our role as spectator.
The reflection pulls us into the red or bluish world and as we look at the piece
we watch our self watching us in color.
This analytic process asks questions about reality and art with the same
intensity, and this is the zone in my memory where your pieces are stored.

They come back from time to time and sometimes when I kiss my kids
good night.

Erwin Wurm
Vienna, May 27th 2004

List of the works

All the paintings are : oil on plastic and canvas.

Sébastien de Ganay portraits & sculptures

Sébastien de Ganay was born in France in 1962, lived all his childhood in Argentina, did his graduate studies at Columbia University with a BA in Political Science and a MA in Film. He has lived and worked in Austria since 1999. He has had many solo shows since 1991, in England with Richard Salmon, in France with Jacqueline Rabouan Moussion, in Austria with Sylvia Steinek and his second show at Häusler Contemporary in Germany is in September 2004.

Introductory text by **Richard Dailey**
Interview by **Benedikt Ledebur**
A letter to Sébastien by **Erwin Wurm**

The artist dedicates this book to Katharina, Emile and Alma, *and wishes to thank:* Mélanie and Christophe, Günter, Toby and Anna, Ariane, Gretchen and Howard, Edmond, Alix, Hans, Anna J., Franz, Erwin, Ferdinand, Letizia, India, Clotilde, Gwendoline, Peter, Marie Thérèse, Mathias, Hélène, Margaux, Philippine, Jean-Louis, Rudolph, Benedikt, Selina, Uriel, Richard S., Richard D., Matthias, Philipp, Georg, Gerold, Siegrun, Andrea, Martin W., Martin G., Michel, Christl, Daniel, Hugo, Markus, Bruno, Pierre A., Miguel, Frédéric, Marie, Adrian, Franzi, Herr Ried, Bertrand, Soo, Shin, Sylvia, Carole, Wolfgang, Christa, Marina, Buz, Maria-Pia, Nathalie, Giuseppe, Jimmy, Isabelle.

Artistic direction and layout: Christophe Boutin
Photos: Richard Dailey, Bertrand Stark, Georg Leutner, Xavier Grandsard

Translation: Matthias Goldmann

First edition limited to 1000 copies
Printed and bound in Spain

© 2004 Sébastien de Ganay, the authors and onestar press

This monograph was made possible with the help of **Häusler Contemporary**, **Galerie Sylvia Steinek** and **Richard Salmon**.

ISBN: 2-915359-07-5

onestar press
16, rue Trolley de Prévaux
75013 Paris France
info@onestarpress.com
www.onestarpress.com

onestar press monos - *monographs by artists*
1: Hans Schabus
2: Sébastien de Ganay